A Room with a Differentiated View

A Room with a Differentiated View

How to Serve ALL Children as Individual Learners

JOANNE YATVIN

HEINEMANN  PORTSMOUTH, NH

HEINEMANN
A division of Reed Elsevier Inc.
361 Hanover Street
Portsmouth, NH 03801–3912
www.heinemann.com

Offices and agents throughout the world

The author and publisher wish to thank those who have generously given permission to reprint borrowed material:

Excerpts on pages 26, 53, 54, 59, 64, 65, 71, 87, 91, 103, 114, 115, and 129 from *Learning Language Through Communication: A Functional Perspective* by R. R. Allen, Kenneth L. Brown, and Joanne Yatvin. Copyright © 1986 by Wadsworth, Inc. Published by Wadsworth Publishing Company. Reprinted by permission of the author.

Library of Congress Cataloging-in-Publication Data
Yatvin, Joanne.
   A room with a differentiated view : how to serve all children as individual learners / Joanne Yatvin.
        p. cm.
   Includes bibliographical references and index.
   ISBN 0-325-00669-5 (alk. paper)
   1. Individualized instruction. 2. Mixed ability grouping in education. I. Title.

LB1031.Y38 2004
371.39'4—dc22   2004008511

Editor: Lois Bridges
Production: Lynne Reed
Cover design: Jenny Jensen Greenleaf
Cover photographs: © Getty Images 24125, 41036, and 41120
Text design: Jenny Jensen Greenleaf
Typesetter: Gina Poirier
Manufacturing: Steve Bernier

Printed in the United States of America on acid-free paper
08   07   06   05   RRD   2   3   4   5

For my brave and
beautiful daughter,

LILLIAN AKED YATVIN

Contents

Acknowledgments

No writer writes alone. No teacher teaches alone. We are surrounded by a crowd of shadowy mentors, whispering their knowledge in our ears and re-enacting their experience in our mind's eye. I think this is especially true for me. So much of my own eighteen years of teaching was trial and error, and I had so little time to reflect on it. But I did learn from the books I read and from the teachers I worked with. I regret that I cannot remember all the writers who helped me to understand teaching, learning, and children so I could acknowledge them here. But I do know that I was powerfully influenced by the writings of Charles Dickens, John Dewey, Sylvia Ashton Warner, John Holt, Douglas Barnes, Lucianne Bond Carmichael, and, above all, Frank Smith. I humbly thank them all for their wisdom.

My most important mentors, however, were the teachers at Crestwood School in Madison, Wisconsin, where I was principal from 1974 to 1988. Several of them are named in this book in vignettes describing differentiated instruction as it should be done. Later, I also learned a great deal from the teachers at Cottrell and Bull Run Schools in Boring, Oregon, and from Pam Perrin, a remarkable first grade teacher at Hazeldale School in Beaverton, Oregon.

The actual writing of this book was made possible by my husband, Milton Yatvin, who kept telling me for years that I should put my experiences into a book and who, once I'd started it, pushed me toward my desk every morning and took over running the household so I didn't have to. I also thank my children (in alphabetical order) Alan, Bruce, Lillian, and Richard who have always cheered me on.

In addition, I would like to thank my editor, Lois Bridges, for her steadfast direction and encouragement and my production editor, Lynne Reed, for taking over the detail work I have no talent for.

Introduction

In my very first teaching assignment, unskilled and inexperienced, I faced the need to differentiate literacy instruction. What was I to do with twenty-eight third graders—about a third of them struggling with reading—and one set of basals? Although the plan I came up with was clumsy and worked no magic, it made it possible for all of us to get through the year. I divided those who were readers into two groups of manageable size and took each group through the basal at its own pace. I borrowed an outdated set of second-grade basals from another teacher for my strugglers. And I used the public library as the source of beginning books for my nonreaders.

Over the ensuing years, like most teachers, I learned through trial and error how to provide more appropriate work and materials for most of my students. And, also like them, I harbored guilty feelings about those bright kids I failed to challenge and the few bewildered ones I couldn't reach and teach. Thinking I might do better with younger—and then older—students, I changed grade levels several times.

Still, the concept of "differentiated instruction" seemed beyond my grasp. It suggested planning several different reading and writing lessons every day for the range of ordinary students' abilities and regularly doing one-on-one tutoring for students at either end of the ability spectrum. In contrast, an individualized reading program I'd read about sounded easy. No planning, no tutoring, just talking with kids about the books they were reading. I tried it, and it almost did me in. Not only did I have to buy more than fifty paperback books with my own money to supplement the meager classroom library the school supplied, but I also had to read and remember them all in order to discuss them with my students. Unfortunately, I kept forgetting details and mixing up plots. Most of the time I couldn't even think of questions to ask. At the end of the year, I looked at the record of my students' learning and the side effects for me, and decided that individualized reading wasn't worth doing again.

When I became an elementary principal a few years later, I began to see teachers at work who were cleverer and better organized than I had been. They were meeting a wide range of student needs by using just a few different books at a time in flexible reading groups and letting students find their own interests and levels of competence in writing. Some of their assignment and monitoring systems were complex, but others were fairly simple. Some teachers appeared to be working very hard, but others seemed to be doing it all with a wave of the hand. I also saw teachers who were just beginning to differentiate class and group activities in small ways, dipping their toes into the water, so to speak, and finding that the process was manageable and rewarding if they didn't go too fast and didn't make too many changes all at once.

That was twenty-five years ago. Since then, I have worked closely with roughly fifty teachers and visited the classrooms of many more. The practice of differentiated instruction has become more sophisticated and subtle, as younger teachers have learned to apply all the fine points they've been taught. Today's teachers understand—as I didn't—that you don't have to have different materials and assignments for each student. The secret is in how students make varied use of the learning opportunities available, not in multiple curricula.

Still, practicing differentiated instruction today is harder than it should be. Instead of being encouraged to use all the knowledge, skills, and insights they have made their own, many teachers are being told by policy makers to employ materials and methods they don't believe in and to use them for all students at the same time and in the same way.

Faced with directives and the unshakable certainty of people in power, what should teachers do? Will they get into trouble if their ways of teaching don't blend with the school's approved methods and materials? How can they ignore the needs of students who are bored, slow in learning, or just different? What will happen to them if their students' test scores aren't as high as those of more compliant teachers?

I can't promise that this book will answer all questions and solve all problems. In truth, differentiating instruction is harder than standardizing it. Treating each child as a capable learner and a valuable class member is time consuming. Yet, the job is doable, as thousands of teachers demonstrate every day, and it gets easier with practice and an accumulation of materials and tasks that can be used in various ways. This book is designed to help teachers figure out why, when, and how to differentiate; it also provides lots of solid examples of what other teachers are doing. As a realist, I am very aware of the highly visible, demanding, and dangerous stage teachers perform on today. Not only do I care about optimizing students' learning, but also about optimizing teachers' survival—or, more accurately, teachers' triumph over whatever obstacles block their way.

This book is divided into three sections. The first includes a brief overview of the history and theory behind differentiated instruction, because I believe you can't do a good job with anything unless you know what others have tried in the past and why you are joining their parade. But the main focus in the section is on the basics of differentiation: what teachers need to know, have, and do to get started. In part, successful differentiation depends on the physical aspects of the classroom and the structure of its operation. But it also depends on developing an ongoing interaction between assessment and instruction and devising solid, simple ways of helping students learn the common knowledge base they all need. The second section is an examination of high-level differentiation practices, organized around the various constituents of the language arts: reading, writing, drama, poetry, and projects. The emphasis in these chapters is on students' differentiating their own learning within the supportive framework the teacher has provided. The third and final section includes a chapter about differentiating for students at both ends of the ability spectrum: the plodders and the zoomers. Although strategies for teaching these students are not substantively different from those used with the mid-range of students in the classroom, both more leeway and more support are necessary. The book concludes with a chapter about the teacher, her preservation and growth as a differentiator, with an emphasis on becoming the kind of teacher who does it all with "a wave of the hand."

Readers will find that there are few references to research findings and other authors' views of differentiated instruction in this book. Although I am certain I have borrowed many ideas from innovative thinkers in my own long journey as a teacher, my intention was to write from my own experiences and those of the teachers I have known. My fear was that if I got too scholarly or too dependent on the theories of others, I would lose some of the authenticity of real teachers and real students struggling to find meaning, value, and beauty in their school lives. Inside their classrooms is where I hope to take you.

A Short History of Differentiated Instruction

The story of differentiated instruction is a brief and recently written chapter in the history of education. Only in the past fifty years have there been any concerted efforts to provide teaching that is tailored to the learning needs of each student in a classroom. Through the centuries the primary purpose of education was to hand down a fixed body of knowledge from the old to the young, and as long as that purpose prevailed, there was no need for differentiation. The teacher's job was to present all students with the same information and the students' part was to assimilate that information and repeat it back on demand. Under such circumstances a "one size fits all" approach was not unreasonable. Most of the children of privilege could hold up their end of the bargain, and poor children weren't educated anyway. It was only in the twentieth century, when education came to be viewed as the birthright of all children and learning viewed as thinking, creating, and problem solving, that the notion of differentiating instruction got thrown into the instructional mix.

American Traditions in Education

As new as differentiation is, its philosophical roots run deep in American soil. Our traditions of freedom, independence, and pioneering have always encouraged Americans to reinvent their institutions as they went along, with little attention to what others had done in the past. In colonial times schools were founded to deliver religious instruction, but since religions and their beliefs about raising children differed considerably from colony to colony, so did schools. As America expanded, various colonies and sections of the land made changes in their schools to reflect the kinds of work being done locally and the economic status of the population. In many places private schools for children of the wealthy and apprenticeship training for those of the working class rose alongside common schools for the middle class, but only in one or two colonies were there free schools for the poor. In each type of school the form of education followed its supposed function for that particular social class.

In what is known as the National Period, commencing in the late eighteenth century, states began to put education into their constitutions. Since national leaders such as Thomas Jefferson saw education as the cornerstone of the new democracy, schools became not only more democratic in their acceptance of students, but also more secular, practical, and civic minded in their curricula. A variety of academies were established for different types of education: military schools, seminaries, manual labor schools, music schools, schools for young ladies of good families, and others. But not until public high schools became widespread in the mid-nineteenth century did any institution offer any curricular choices to its students.

High Schools

High schools sprang up in urban areas where populations were mixed, and there was an obvious need to bring together students of different backgrounds with different academic aspirations and needs. One strong pressure on urban high schools was the growth of industrialism, which for the first time required a large number of workers to be able to read, write, and figure in order to do their jobs and manage their everyday lives. Another was the large and rapid influx of European immigrants into eastern cities; these new arrivals and their children needed to learn a new language and fit into an unfamiliar society.

In rural areas high schools came more slowly. The western movement of the mid-nineteenth century produced small towns and isolated settlements where one-room, one-teacher schoolhouses had to serve the full range of ages and abilities of resident children. Until those areas grew into cities or, at least, connected communities, which in many cases did not happen until well into the twentieth century, they had no high schools.

In attempting to meet the varied needs of students, schools developed a number of strategies that were more pragmatic than theoretical. In urban areas the public schools chose to keep poor, foreign-born and working-class children separated from the children of prosperous and established families. To do that, they created new sections of classes, or tracks, for the newcomers, where less demanding and more practical curricula could be taught. Rural schools, having both fewer students and fewer teachers, focused on a core curriculum of basics for everyone. However, the rural school experience was differentiated by students' age and aptitude. The young ones were pampered while the older ones were expected to be care-takers and tutors. Students left school when they had mastered the curriculum or given up hope of mastering it. Those few who showed academic promise were sent off to boarding schools in more populated areas or encouraged to continue learning on their own, assisted by their teachers or parents.

The Influence of Educational Theory

At the same time that demographics were determining the nature of American schooling, educational theory was beginning to influence poli-cies of curriculum and instruction. Jean Jacques Rousseau, a European philosopher, introduced radical and romantic ideas about education in his book *Emile* (1755) (see Boyd 1957), a fictional odyssey of one young man's education in the company of an enlightened tutor. Rousseau asserted that education should follow the natural growth patterns of children, protect them from the corruptions of civilization, nurture their native abilities, and allow them to follow their interests. He believed that childhood existed for its own sake and should not be manipulated to serve the purposes of adults or society. He thought that children should not even be taught to read; they would teach themselves, if so inclined.

Blending nicely with the ideas of European romanticism was the twentieth-century American concept of progressivism, developed prima-rily by John Dewey. Like Rousseau, Dewey emphasized the centrality of the child in the educational process, but he went further to define the school as the surrogate for the real world. As adults live their lives in that world, so should children live theirs in school. Although Dewey's philosophy of education was broader and more complicated than Rousseau's, it was also more realistic, intended to better the lives of real children in real schools. At the same time, Dewey's proposals were less utilitarian than those of the nineteenth-century educators who had organized the schools by social class. Dewey wanted to change society through education, making it more democratic by providing both practical and intellectual studies for all students. He believed that children learned best through active involvement in work they perceived as authentic, important, and interesting. He also wanted teaching to be more humane, centered on the well-being of children rather than on the demands of the curriculum.

The Early Twentieth Century

Surprisingly, Rousseau's and Dewey's ideas, much debated in intellectual circles and disseminated at the best universities, had slight impact on public schools in the first half of the twentieth century. From the 1930s through the 1950s, the only official concessions elementary schools made to the needs of students were ability groups within classrooms, and the only connections to life in the real world were home economics classes for girls and shop classes for boys. An add-on course called vocational guidance, taught in the upper elementary grades, was the students' sole exposure to the world of work. Although high schools appeared to offer more differentiation through vocational offerings and different math and English courses for students of varying abilities, the primary fact of high school life was still social, economic, ethnic, and racial tracking.

Mid-Twentieth-Century Concepts of Differentiation

In the prosperous post–World War II days of the 1950s, textbooks were plentiful and they became the curriculum. Every elementary classroom had several sets, one for each subject, along with workbooks for most subjects. The daily routine was one subject after another for about an hour at a time, with the most important ones, such as reading and math, always taught in the morning. Minor subjects, such as health, got their hour once or twice a week. Teachers actually did little teaching. Their job was to present directions and assignments, correct work, issue grades, and, of course, maintain order. Students read textbooks, answered questions, and completed worksheets. Every week or so there was a test. Neither teachers nor students were expected to express ideas or opinions. Since Title I did not yet exist and special education was reserved for the mentally handicapped, ability grouping was the only way to differentiate instruction within the classroom. If students got too far behind, they were retained in the same grade for another year. In the upper grades of any K–8 school, it was not uncommon to find as much as a quarter of a class a year or more older than they should have been, as the result of retentions in lower grades. Ironically, perhaps, schools hailed retention as a form of differentiation: "giving students more time to master the curriculum."

New Directions

True differentiated instruction, in the sense of trying to meet the needs of children without separating them from their peers or punishing them, was born in the 1960s and took off in several directions at once. One direction was a movement called "individualized instruction" that, like earlier ability grouping, operated by varying the time students spent in learning the same material. In most individualized classrooms students were given packets for a unit of work that they completed on their own. Some individualized instruction schools were ungraded, since students were promoted to a higher grade without physically moving to another classroom whenever they finished the packets of the previous grade. Because individualized instruction entailed little actual teaching, and because most of the children and adolescents involved did not have the skills or self-discipline to go it alone, the movement turned out to be short lived. Today packets of work for students to complete on their own are still common in many classrooms, but they are usually accompanied by teacher instruction and group activities.

Another direction for differentiation in the sixties was the "open classroom," which became quite fashionable in private schools and suburban public schools. The open classroom owed a lot to the ideas of A. S. Neill, who founded a private school named Summerhill in England and wrote about it in a book of the same name. At Summerhill students made all group and individual decisions, not only about what, where, and how they would study but also about whether they would study at all. They also engaged in physical work, such as building things and taking care of animals and plants, that was appropriate to the school's rural setting. Although open classrooms in the United States were not quite so free, they did offer lots of choices and lots of hands-on activities. In a sense, teachers of open classrooms were teaching twenty-five separate curricula. They had to be exceptionally skillful and well organized to keep everyone working productively. But since many of the idealistic teachers drawn to open class-rooms were also young and inexperienced, they often did not have the skills to carry it off. Many students foundered, and the movement dwindled and died within a decade.

A type of individualized reading also emerged around this time. Students were allowed to choose their own books, pace themselves, and demonstrate their fluency and comprehension through conferences with the teacher and some form of writing. Teachers were not burdened with planning for group instruction, but they still had to work hard to read all the books, get around to all their students, and keep records of progress. Individualized reading—as it was then conceived—also soon died out. The programs asked too little of students and too much of teachers. On the other hand, more structured and less labor intensive forms of individualized reading flourish in many classrooms today, and students make solid progress in them.

Some small-scale differentiation practices also originated in the sixties: shorter or customized spelling lists, homework assignments with "extra credit" options, projects and writing assignments geared to varying levels of difficulty, predetermined grades tied to particular amounts of work, "fun" activities students could do if they finished their class work early. Most of these practices have proved relatively durable because they do not require teachers to do a lot of additional planning, instruction, monitoring, or assessment. In addition, they make teachers feel virtuous, and capable students and their parents feel they are getting a high-quality education.

The Rise of Constructivism

In the 1970s new concepts of differentiation appeared as the results of advances in psychology and the rise of a constructivist philosophy of learning. Educators came to believe that motivation is the key to children's learning and that learning means building one's own mental frameworks. Among constructivist teachers, a whole language approach to teaching literacy became wildly popular. Although whole language has had different manifestations in the hands of different teachers, philosophically it is the belief that reading and writing are intimately connected to competence in oral language and knowledge of literature and the world. Thus, all components of literacy develop together, each supporting the other, though not all at the same rate or with the same intensity. With its workshop approach to learning, its broad array of choices in materials and activities, its frequent opportunities for collaborative work, and its emphasis on teachers as coaches, whole language put differentiated instruction at the center of the classroom curriculum for the first time. Although the whole language approach never became as widespread in this country as its detractors would have us believe, it was prominent enough and respected enough to dominate educational thinking, writing, and policy making for the past thirty years. Even now, at a time when whole language is out of favor with policy makers, it continues to be popular with teachers who see the bene-fits of motivation, high-quality literature, authentic activities, and variety for their students.

In the 1980s several new theories and innovative practices related to differentiated instruction were introduced. Through professional books and journals, conferences, and workshops, teachers became familiar with "multiple intelligences," " cooperative learning," "learning styles," and the "integrated curriculum"; many took up the challenge to adopt and adapt such practices in their classrooms. In addition, changing laws and prac-tices in special education brought disabled children of all kinds into regular classrooms to be educated with their age peers under the concept of "inclusion." Although these students received some specialized instruc-tion outside the classroom and came with "individualized educational plans"; classroom teachers were still expected to do most of the instruc-tion and to help students make whatever social and emotional adjust-ments were needed. At the other end of the spectrum, special programs were developed for "gifted" children, taking them out of regular class-rooms for time periods from an hour to a day each week. Since gifted students were usually expected to make up the classroom work they missed, these pull-out programs were not popular with the students in them or their teachers.

Supporting all these changes in classroom structure and teaching were a deepening public understanding of the distinctive nature of childhood and a growing appreciation of the diversity in American life. As the twen-tieth century wound down, the focus of education was shifting from the mastery of the curriculum to the development of the child, with psycholo-gists, teachers, and parents beginning to understand that children's abili-ties and interests grow in different directions and at different rates, and that the cultures children live in greatly affect how they learn. In addition, new teachers coming into the profession during this period had had a different kind of professional preparation, one that emphasized the human dimensions of learning and teaching as well as the technical ones.

And, to some extent, these teachers were a new breed. No longer was teaching a default profession for people with limited options. Knowing full well that the work was hard, the pay mediocre, and the chances for glory few, young men and women chose their profession for its promise of opportunities to serve, nurture, and love other people's children.

Twenty-First-Century Trends

As we move into the twenty-first century, the interest in differentiated instruction is greater than ever, but the forces that drive that interest have changed and are far apart in their philosophies. The major impetus comes from believers in standards and accountability. In their view schools should use alternative classroom configurations, teaching methods, and student activities to help struggling learners score high on standardized tests. They use "prevention" and "intervention" as key words to signal more and different instruction for children who are not making it in ordinary classroom programs. The other group pushing for differentiation believes in the uniqueness of every learner. These people accept the concept of each child's individuality underlying the late-twentieth-century school practices mentioned earlier, and want to see it brought to life in regular classrooms for all students. They believe that instruction should be matched to the particular learning needs, interests, talents, personality, and home background of each student. The goal of education in this context is the optimal development of a child as the foundation for professional success and personal happiness. Such a goal is certainly different from the old one of the transmission of knowledge, but it is also different from the goal of standardization, which is to produce a high, but uniform, level of learning in all students for the benefit (primarily the economic benefit) of society. While these two aims are not mutually exclusive, they are different enough to engender separate, distinct strands of differentiation in the school curriculum.

The Position of This Book

In reviewing all the things differentiated instruction means now and has meant in the past, I have laid out the range of possibilities this book will cover and, at the same time, suggested its limits. I will describe as many as I can of the ways teachers have thought of to manipulate time, space, grouping practices, materials, human resources, and instructional techniques to meet the needs of their students. On the other hand, I am not going to reintroduce any schemes schools have used over the years to segregate children by class, race, or ethnicity. Nor will I offer any strategies that label children as winners or losers within their classrooms. At the heart of my own philosophy of education is the belief that children learn best in a community of equals where they continually teach and learn from each other and produce in concert what no one of them could produce alone. This is the ideal I choose to keep foremost as I discuss ideas for differentiating literacy instruction. Still, because I am aware that the reasons for differentiating and the ways available to do so are at least partly determined by time, place, politics, and clientele, I will make every effort to offer suggestions that can serve a variety of school contexts in the twenty-first century.

References

BOYD, W. 1962. *Emile of Jean Jacques Rousseau.* New York: Teachers College Press.

BUTTS, R. F., AND CREMIN, L. 1953. *A History of Education in American Culture.* New York: Holt.

CURTI, M. 1959. *The Social Ideas of American Educators.* Lanham, MD: Littlefield, Adams & Co.

DEWEY, J. 2001. *The School and Society & The Child and the Curriculum.* Mineola, NY: Dover Publications, Inc.

GRAVES, F. P. 1925. *A History of Education in Modern Times.* New York: MacMillan.

NEIL, A. S. 1960. *Summerhill: A Radical Approach to Child Rearing.* New York: Hart.

Using Classroom Space
and Time Differently

Although I'm certain that a determined teacher can differentiate instruction anywhere, under any conditions, having a classroom where time, space, materials, procedures, and resources are well organized can make the job much easier. In this chapter I will discuss the various aspects of a differentiated classroom as they differ from a conventional classroom. At the same time I hope to make clear that there is no one right way. Just as classrooms differ in their shapes, sizes, and amenities, schools differ in what they can supply and teachers differ in their feelings about clutter, movement, and noise.

Using Space Efficiently

Teachers who want to differentiate instruction need to think about differentiating space in their classrooms beforehand. When large numbers of students are engaged in different types of work at the same time—some of it interactive and noisy, and some of it solitary and quiet—they need elbow room, boundaries, and neutral passing zones to minimize distractions. Theoretically, the amount of classroom space needed decreases at higher grade levels because older students are less active and more self-disciplined than younger ones. In reality, however, upper-grade classes tend to be larger. So, creating places for differentiated work can be difficult at any grade if a classroom is small or crowded. Teachers will have to do what they have always done: improvise, which means having areas do double and even triple duty. But first, let's consider the basic space needs for a differentiated classroom.

Every student needs a place for solitary work, thinking, and storage of personal possessions. Traditionally, this place has been a desk. But because student desks come in different widths and heights, often with slanted tops, they are not very easily pushed together for group work. If you have a choice, choose tables—round ones. They are cheaper for a school to buy than desks and more flexible for students to use. A round table can provide personal space for four students and small-group space for six or eight. Also, a table for four takes up less floor space than four desks, leaving more room for specialized activity areas. When a classroom is furnished with tables, students can keep their personal belongings in plastic tubs on shelves, in hanging bags, or in cubicles.

In a differentiated classroom, students also need space for specialized activities, such as doing research, painting a mural, practicing a play, binding a book, or reading aloud to a partner. In the lower grades there should be a large open area, preferably carpeted, for children to sit on the floor, but there should also be some uncarpeted floor space or large tables for painting and construction. At any grade level a classroom library area is a must, along with a small comfortable reading-writing-thinking place equipped with a dictionary, a thesaurus, paper, writing tools, and at least one computer. Another computer might be placed in a technical work area along with a paper cutter, a spiral binding machine, and, if the school is prosperous, a letter stencil machine, a scanner, and a desktop copier.

The teacher needs some differentiated space too. Like students, she might be better served by a table than a desk. Unlike them, she needs enough room to keep her computer, current materials, supplies, and student records close at hand. That means shelves, one or more file cabinets, and probably an extra table close by. She also needs a student-sized table to meet with small groups or individuals. Psychologically, it's good for teachers to eliminate their desks, which are traditional seats of power and isolation. And since teachers who differentiate move around the classroom a lot to see how students are doing, they probably will do better with an armless rolling chair than a traditional desk chair.

What I haven't mentioned yet are the centers for math, science, art, and so on that are commonly found in elementary classrooms. These are intended to provide curricular variety, hands-on activities, and a change of pace for young children, but they do not ordinarily provide differentiated tasks. I see good reasons to continue using them in primary grades, but in higher grades it seems to me that it's better to have more generalized areas that can be used for a variety of differentiated activities rather than ones dedicated only to a specific type and level of subject matter.

Beyond using the available classroom space for various purposes, you may have to ask yourself if anything now taking up room can be eliminated. I have observed that many teachers store things in their classrooms that do not need to be there: books not currently in use, AV equipment, old curriculum guides, leftover student projects, and extra supplies. I have also seen classrooms where student desks or tables were arranged to take up more room than they needed to, presumably to aid discipline. These are space problems that can be solved if you are willing to trust students more and store some things outside the classroom. Another way to economize on space is to go vertical. Many teachers have lofts built in their classrooms and find them to be lifesavers. Others reserve high shelves and cabinets for the things only they need to reach, leaving lower places for student materials.

Once the various activity places have been situated, the classroom furniture has been arranged, and the unused materials stored more efficiently, you may find there is enough room to have the passing zones and boundaries previously mentioned. We'd like students to be able to move about the room without stumbling over others, and we'd like to insulate working groups and individuals from distracting sights and sounds. If each area has its own expectations for behavior, boundaries will help to reinforce those ideas of order. In the lower grades, boundaries work better if they're concrete, such as bookcases framing the reading-writing-thinking corner; while in upper grades boundaries work just as well when they exist only in students' minds.

Organizing Time

Dividing the school day into large and flexible blocks of time provides the foundation for differentiated instruction. Students need long stretches of time not only because they are doing different amounts and kinds of work, but also because they are integrating material from different subjects, delving deeply into a variety of information sources, and working out sustained and complex projects. The teacher also needs blocks of time to check on how students are progressing, confer with those who need help, and plan with those who are ready to move on.

Yet, time is a factor that most teachers have little control over. Typically, someone else decides when the class goes to lunch, recess, gym, and music, and when struggling students go for specialized instruction. The effects on classrooms, whether they are conventional or differentiated, can be devastating. Some teachers tell me that they are lucky if they have their whole class together for an hour a day, and I have been in classrooms where large numbers of students have been pulled out for one thing or another while the teacher was teaching a core subject. Although struggling readers, writers, or English language learners deserve supplementary instruction or tutoring, they also need to be part of their class, getting directions and doing major literacy activities with their peers. Hoping they'll figure out what the class is doing and catch up with the activity when they come back defies common sense. The reason these students need supplementary instruction in the first place is because they're not good at figuring things out or catching up. Ideally, elementary teachers and all their students should have two literacy blocks every day of at least ninety minutes each. Middle schoolers need blocks, too, but rarely get them. By combining language arts and social studies into one course, middle schools can provide at least a two-period block of ninety to one hundred minutes every day.

When school principals set up schedules for their teachers, they are not intentionally working to minimize and fragment classroom instruction. They are just trying to fit in all the special classes and services available, and they can't possibly give all teachers the periods they want. At the same time, principals often don't realize the harmful effects of their decisions on classrooms, or they think there is no better way to do scheduling. To gain some control over time, I suggest teachers participate in the scheduling process, not as individuals but as teams willing to alternate physical education and music among themselves and move their language arts block to a time when another team wants special classes. When a school staff works together on a schedule, they can usually find ways to improve it substantially.

There is more to using time well than having blocks, however. Blocks have to be broken into activity segments that suit the attention span and social impulses of students, which of course vary by age, temperament, and habit. Although twenty-minute segments for young children and forty-minute ones for middle schoolers are good rules of thumb, there is lots of variation in the needs of particular classes and individuals. You need to find out just how long your students can work at one type of job without getting bored or restless. Start with that amount of time and build upward toward a time span that is necessary to complete an activity. Adjusting time for the few students who work slowly or those who finish quickly and want to move on is part of the business of differentiation. That can be done by offering several options for things to do when the required work is finished. You should change these options often and remind students of their choices every day until they go to them automatically.

Students who consistently have trouble completing their work in the time allocated may also benefit from changes in the amount of work expected, short breaks, or the opportunity to work with a partner. Contrary to what we might expect, other students do not resent such modifications as long as they understand similar ones will be available to them if they need them.

Making time adjustments is always easier if the classroom curriculum is integrated—that is, when literacy learning is a part of every subject and there are few limitations on how independent work time may be used. Without distorting the logical progression in the math curriculum, for example, you can have students applying math skills in science and social studies activities. And almost anything we want students to learn about reading, writing, or speaking can be taught through social studies or science subject matter. Although teachers need to draw the class together at certain times for specific types of direct instruction, the rest of the classroom day can be used flexibly as group and independent work time, with the teacher emphasizing the various projects and assignments in progress that students may choose to work on. Two examples of daily schedules for different grade levels are offered in Figure 2-1 to make clear how such a schedule can be integrated, flexible, and specific all at once. In these schedules, a literacy block may be interrupted for recess or lunch, as long as that time is not subtracted from the eighty- to ninety-minute block. Subjects and special classes can be moved around, too, and the block times can be moved forward or backward to avoid having fifteen-minute time spans in between. The purpose of these illustrations is to show you that literacy blocks are possible, not to prescribe when subject matter should be taught.

Let me say one more thing about time that is obvious but not usually considered in making up a schedule. The teacher's time is not the same as the students' time. Children of all ages need periodic contact with the teacher to show her what they've been doing, ask questions, and be reminded of appropriate behavior. These things are easy enough to do when students are all engaged in independent work, harder when you are trying to instruct small groups at the same time. I suggest five-to-ten minute breaks between group meetings so you can attend to students' needs and catch your breath. Thus, in an hour literacy block, you would be able to meet with only two groups. That is one reason why I have stated that blocks should be ninety minutes in length.

Elementary Grade Schedule		Middle School Schedule	
8:30–9	Morning Routines	8:30–8:45	Homeroom Routines

9–10:30	Literacy Block
	    Long Term Groups
	    Writing
	    Silent Reading
	    Projects
		8:45–10:45	Block for Literacy and
			Social Studies
			or Math and Science

		10:45–11:45	Special Subject—PE, Music, Foreign Language, Art
10:30–10:45	Recess		
10:45–11:45	Math, PE, Music, or Library	11:45–12:15	Lunch
11:45–12:30	Lunch and Recess	12:15–2:15	Block for Math and Science or Literacy and Social Studies
12:30–1:30	Music, Library, PE, or Math		
1:30–1:45	Recess	2:15–3:15	Special Subject—PE, Music, Foreign Language, or Art

1:45–3:15	Literacy Block
	    Temporary Groups
	    Class Story
	    Writing
	    Silent Reading
	    Cleanup		

		3:15	Dismissal
3:15	Dismissal		

FIGURE 2-1: *Primary Grade and Middle School Schedules*

Equipping for Differentiation

Let's move on now to the equipment teachers need for differentiated instruction. Classroom differentiation flourishes most readily when students have available the variety and quantity of tools adults have in the real world. They should have opportunities to create and construct projects as well as to read and write. Some of the necessary tools have already been mentioned in the section on classroom space, but I will name them again here along with others I think are important. Recognizing that I am suggesting several items that many schools cannot afford, I have listed things in the order of importance, but also, roughly, in the order of cost. You may stop reading when you mentally run out of money. If your school is prosperous or its parent organization is good at fund-raising, you may be able to add some items at the end of the list to your classroom.

chalkboard or dry-erase board	camera
pocket chart	2 Dictaphone-type recorders
2 easels and chart paper	spiral binding machine
overhead projector	digital camera
teacher computer	desktop copier
printer	scanner
4 student computers	camcorder
paper cutter	letter stencil machine

Of course, there are many other useful things I could have listed, such as wall maps and tape recorders with headphones, but these are so common in classrooms that I didn't think it necessary. Conversely, I listed the chalkboard because that prosaic item seems to be disappearing from elementary classrooms in my vicinity. Chalkboards are often covered over with bulletin boards because some children have chalk dust allergies, and they have not been replaced with anything because administrators figure that there is an overhead projector to write on. In my opinion, if it is necessary to remove chalkboards from classrooms, a school should replace at least one section of them with dry-erase boards. Both the teacher and the students need some public place to write impromptu messages, reminders, and lists.

I also listed student computers, even though most classrooms have at least one, because some of the schools I visit have pooled almost all of theirs in a computer room, thus severely limiting their availability to students. This is a mistake, because you can't predict when a child will need a computer for something important. The classroom printer is listed for a similar reason. Some schools connect classroom computers to a printer in the library or another central location, which saves money but also discourages productivity. Children do not like to have to wait or travel to see what their work looks like printed out.

When it comes to teaching-learning materials that are important for differentiating instruction, I will follow the same format I used for equipment. Again, you may stop reading when the cost becomes more than your school can bear.

fiction books

nonfiction books

basal readers

student dictionaries

reference books

topical picture file

adult dictionaries

magazines, comic books, and other forms of popular culture

daily newspapers

children's thesauruses

unabridged dictionary

As you can see, the materials listed above are fewer and more generalized than the pieces of equipment identified earlier. Not all the types of appropriate books appear here. The important point about books is that there should be lots of them, on a wide variety of topics, and covering a range of reading levels. It is difficult for an outsider to say just how many books a classroom library should have. A lot depends on whether books are likely to be in children's homes, how well stocked and available the school library is, and whether or not the public library is convenient. You need enough so that students can always find something recreational they want to read and so they don't have to wait in line for a reference book.

There are a few specifics I want to emphasize, however. Although basal readers—above, below, and at grade level—should be available in the classroom, you don't have to have one for every student. Even if you are required to teach from an adopted basal series, you need only enough books for a small group; different groups should have different books, so that struggling readers are not plowing through the same stories more able readers have already read and talked about. I have not listed workbooks because I believe they are a waste of students' time and the school's money.

A range of reference books and a picture file should also be available if you plan to differentiate instruction. It is not convenient—and often not possible—to send kids to the library every time they need a piece of information. When it comes to dictionaries, a classroom should have several written for children at that grade level, but not a whole class set except when you are giving direct instruction on how to use a dictionary, and then you can borrow them. Having a couple of adult dictionaries on hand for words that are not in the children's version is also important for differentiation. More capable students will use them a lot, and even average students will occasionally run into a word that is not in a children's dictionary. Thesauruses are important resources, too, but not particularly helpful to children in primary and intermediate grades. Children in these groups are not able to make the fine distinctions that determine in which context a particular word should be used. They will also have trouble finding the right general word categories in the back of the thesaurus. If you do decide to supply thesauruses below middle school, get only a few and go for a children's version.

Popular culture in the form of newspapers, magazines, comic books, and joke books has a place in the classroom as a supplement and an alternative to conventional books. Not only do the artifacts of popular culture motivate reluctant readers and give serious readers a change of pace, they also offer different perspectives on topics of interest to students. Newspapers are not foreign to intermediate and middle school classrooms, since many teachers now order a set of children's weeklies and/or a set of adult dailies. This practice serves the purposes of exposing students to a journalistic style of writing and expanding their knowledge of current places, people, and events. But I think these can be accomplished just as well and more cheaply by having single copies of two or three adult newspapers, which then provide a broader range of information and a comparison of articles. In the same vein, I support as large an array of magazines as the school can afford, rather than class sets of just one. Most classroom magazines should be designed for children (or adolescents), but in the upper grades, students should have the chance to read adult newsmagazines, too

Many teachers, including some who consider themselves traditional teachers, use trade books regularly for instruction. Compared to textbooks, paperback trade books are cheap, and they can be discarded if they don't work out. They are also fairly durable. I've seen many last for ten years or more in a school. A collection of trade books also provides more variety, flexibility, and literary quality than a basal reader. I advise teachers to buy eight to ten copies of a book, pool them with colleagues for greater variety, and store them in a central location. To avoid conflicts over who may use a book and when, some schools set up systems that allocate certain titles to each grade level and also provide many others that are open to any teacher who thinks they are appropriate for her students. Only the grade-restricted titles have to be signed up for in advance. If a school's collection of books is large enough, this system works smoothly and enables teachers to differentiate reading instruction in accordance with students' needs.

Besides having access to a wealth of trade books, students need variety in their classroom library collection. Neither informational nor recreational books should be static. You need to rotate books in and out as students study new topics, as their competence grows, and as their interests change. If you are asking students to do projects or reports on a particular topic, enough books for every student—and a few extra—are necessary. Although the Internet is an invaluable source of all kinds of information, it cannot replace the detail or the personal perspective of books. Ideally, the school librarian will cooperate by lending your classroom a collection of topical books for several weeks at a time. Public libraries in some areas will also gather class-size collections of topical books for teachers and deliver them when requested. If neither option is available, you will have to supply the books yourself by buying or borrowing. This is an opportunity for teachers to team within a school and across schools by forming book collections on various topics and exchanging them with colleagues. Parents can help by donating books and raising funds for new ones and for magazine subscriptions. Book club premiums help, too.

The Goal of Self-Management

Earlier, in discussing the physical aspects of a differentiated classroom, I mentioned the need for behavioral expectations in the areas specially designated for group or individual work. Actually, every place in the classroom should have rules that suit the kind of activity and the number of people likely to be there. But a differentiated classroom needs much more than rules to operate smoothly. Since you will be working with small groups and individuals most of the time when the majority of students are working independently, students will have to manage themselves. Some degree of self-management is a realistic goal even for the youngest and most active students, but it has to be taught and practiced.

The heart of self-management in a classroom is a shared understanding of the way things operate and a sense of community. Since communities take time to develop, you can begin the year by setting a few basic rules, routines, signals, procedures, and devices to be used in the classroom. As soon as a community feeling has been established among students, they should have the opportunity to make whatever changes they think are necessary to suit their needs, learning styles, and personalities.

Rules

Classroom rules should be few and simple. Rules are really only reminders of a whole culture of behavior that everyone understands and agrees to. Some teachers I know present only one rule to their classes. It goes something like "Respect other people at all times," but it means "Don't call names," "Keep your hands and feet to yourself," "Don't borrow other people's pencils without asking," "Wait your turn," and much, much more.

I always caution teachers against having too many rules or rules that are too specific. A long list of rules is hard to remember, and quantity lessens the importance of any one rule in the minds of students. Moreover, overly specific rules invite exceptions. If you say, "All papers on the floor must be picked up by the person whose seat is nearest," that can—and will— be interpreted by some kids to mean that other debris doesn't have to be picked up, or that if a paper lies in the middle of an open space, it isn't anyone's responsibility. So then you will have to make another rule, and another, and still not every situation will be covered.

In a differentiated classroom it's okay to have different levels of rules for different students: a general level where everyone starts, an open level, and a restricted level. For example, those students who have proved themselves responsible might be allowed to go to the bathroom anytime without asking, while those who have left the room too often or stayed away too long might have their number of breaks limited, have to sign out and in, or have to set a timer when they leave. The open and restricted levels work best when negotiated individually with the students for whom they are appropriate. In addition, students who seem to need restrictions should get some warning before you crack down, and they also should be able to work themselves back up to the general level without too much difficulty.

Routines are the ways that the everyday business of the classroom gets done. They are based on efficiency and common sense. Especially in a differentiated classroom, no one wants to waste time on "no-brainers." So, at the beginning of the year the teacher explains and models such things as how to put a proper heading on papers, how to study spelling words, what activities may be engaged in before class formally starts in the morning, and what everyone is expected to do when it's time to clean up. The students practice a routine under teacher scrutiny till everyone gets it right, and then, unless someone comes up with a better way, it is the standard routine from then on.

Rituals differ from routines mainly in their purpose. Although both emphasize and strengthen learning through everyday practice, rituals are designed to bring students together and make them feel like useful, confident, and successful members of the classroom community, rather than to facilitate efficient classroom operation. The vignette on the next page illustrates both the positive feelings and the differentiated learning that can result from a well-planned ritual.

Signals

Signals are attention getters, but they can also be used to trigger a particular routine. A single word, sound, or gesture can tell students to stop work, go to their seats, lower their voices, or get ready for lunch. Using signals saves you time and the wear and tear of having to give complete instructions over and over. Another use for signals is as an agreed-upon code between the teacher and a particular student who needs special reminders. Touching your ear or saying "banana" doesn't embarrass anyone and it can help to forge a bond between you and a hard-to-reach kid.

Procedures

Procedures are more complicated and more variable than routines. They are generalized formats for doing the kinds of activities one might find in a differentiated classroom, such as role playing, research on a history topic, or writing poetry. Teaching a variety of procedures thoroughly is very important in a differentiated classroom, where students are expected to do so much work on their own and to self-regulate their behavior. If students

A Kindergarten Morning Ritual

At 8:25 the kindergartners stream into the hallway outside their large, sunny classroom. Because it is still winter, most are wearing heavy clothing, and it takes them quite a while to undress and stuff their belongings into their lockers. The quick ones are first into the classroom where their teacher, Barbara Wiesner, is busy setting out materials for the day's work. A few children go over to talk to her, but most go straight to the chalkboard where she has printed the "Message for the Day."

Good morning.
Today is Thursday, March 15.
Today is Lillian's birthday.
Today Bruce's mother, Mrs. Harris, will help us work on
*   the computer.*
We will go to music.
We will decorate the pots for our spring plants.
Someone please bring the red handkerchief from my desk.

Several of the children read lines out loud to themselves or a friend nearby. The first two lines are easy since they have been essentially the same since the beginning of the year. Nevertheless, Nancy reads "Tuesday" instead of "Thursday" and Jill corrects her, proving her point by referring to the wall calendar.

Molly spots Bruce's and Lillian's names and runs to tell them they are part of today's message, but she does not wait long enough to read what it says about them. Bruce and Lillian are both smug; they know. By the time they arrive at the chalkboard, other children also know it is Lillian's birthday. The words have become familiar through frequent use. The sentence about Bruce is too hard for the children, so he tells them that his mother's name is Mrs. Harris and she will be at school today. "She's going to 'help us work on the computer,'" reads Jason triumphantly by putting two and two together.

Paul, Marty, and Nina have skipped most of the message and gone right to the secret clue which is always at the end. There they spot "The Word of the Week"—"red"—but they cannot read the word after it. Nina and Marty start out to look for something red, but Paul calls them back. "Look," he says, "that word is 'desk.' Let's look on Ms. Wiesner's desk."

By the time they return with the red handkerchief, now hidden behind Paul's back, all the children are seated on the rug and Ms. Wiesner is in her chair. "Good morning," she smiles. "Let's read today's message." More than a dozen hands shoot up, volunteering to read.

are unsure of how to proceed, work breaks down and the teacher has to scurry around trying to help everyone at once. When a procedure is introduced, it needs to be thoroughly explained and modeled. It is also important for students to see examples of finished products so they know where a procedure will take them. As a class begins to use a procedure, the teacher watches closely and guides them, but ultimately each student has to work through a procedure on his own, modifying it to fit his needs along the way. And since procedures change as tasks change or as students become more proficient, they never become automatic. After an initial tryout, it is a good idea for the teacher to make up and post reminder cards that outline the key points of a procedure for students to consult when they use it again.

Devices are things that remind students where they are in their work, where they've been, and where they are going. Usually devices fall into one of two categories: a record of work accomplished or a guide to completing new work. Records of accomplishment bolster students' self-esteem and encourage them to meet new challenges. They also help teachers and parents to see growth and continuing needs. Guides, both written and visual, support students when they are in unfamiliar territory, freeing them—and the teacher—from the continuing question, "What do I do next?" Teachers have invented so many good devices that I can't begin to describe them all. But I will mention a few of the most popular ones here, and in later chapters I will include others in descriptions of specific activities.

The most common device is an assignment notebook. In a simplified form an assignment book can be used as soon as children can read and write. In first grade, for example, where many teachers write the class news daily with their students and send it home to parents, these sheets can form the basis of a "day book." Either children copy the news in their notebooks or if that is still too difficult for them, the teacher prints out copies to be pasted in. The rest of the sheet has headings and blank spaces for children to add information about work to be done at home, things that need to be brought to school, and reminders about school events. The parent signs the completed page and sends the book back to school the next day. Not only do day books deliver important information to parents, they also provide evidence of children's learning growth and serve as a text for children to read at home. A sample format for a first-grade day book page is shown in Figure 2-2.

From grade three on, students can begin to use more formal assignment notebooks. Some good ones are available commercially for little more than a dollar apiece if you buy them in bulk, but you can always make your own with students. The format is simple: the date, a list of assignments with instructions, and reminders about ongoing projects and upcoming events. As an option, you can put in a place for a parent signature and comments. The advantages of the commercial notebooks are sturdiness, attractiveness, and useful extras, like calendars, weight and measurement tables, and famous quotations.

Other common devices are journals, in which students record events, thoughts, and feelings. Often students are asked to record their reflections on specific classroom activities or books they are reading. Young writers

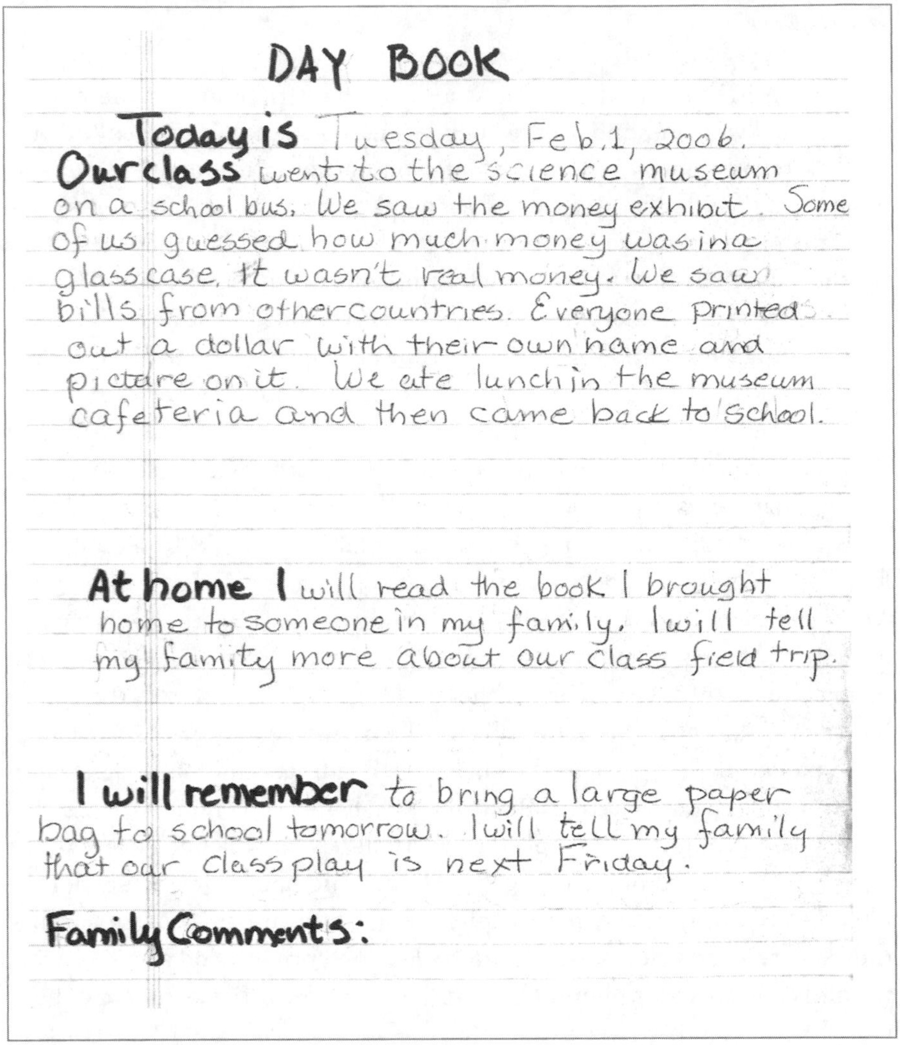

DAY BOOK

Today is Tuesday, Feb. 1, 2006. **Our class** went to the science museum on a school bus. We saw the money exhibit. Some of us guessed how much money was in a glass case. It wasn't real money. We saw bills from other countries. Everyone printed out a dollar with their own name and picture on it. We ate lunch in the museum cafeteria and then came back to school.

At home I will read the book I brought home to someone in my family. I will tell my family more about our class field trip.

I will remember to bring a large paper bag to school tomorrow. I will tell my family that our class play is next Friday.

Family Comments:

FIGURE 2-2: *Day Book*

may also compose stories in their journals or record ideas for stories. Many teachers give prompts for daily journals because some students are inclined to record the same trivia every day.

Graphs and charts are other devices students can use to record the books they've read, the homework they've handed in, their test scores, or behavior ratings. These are concrete evidence of progress—or the lack of it—that helps students to understand their own strengths, weaknesses, and learning patterns. They are also records that parents quickly and easily comprehend.

Checklists for assignments completed are a simple guiding device that keeps students moving and on track. Reminder cards for procedures mentioned earlier, are a bit more sophisticated, helping students remember the steps in a project or a complex assignment. More specialized guides can simplify research by breaking a topic into categories and allocating a certain number of pages for notes about each category. Specialized guides can also be created to help students sort out plot events and the traits of characters in a novel. Other types of specialized guides present formats for giving a speech, writing a short story, or doing an interview. My only concern about guides is that they are sometimes given to students without instruction or modeling. In that sense they are similar to the old individualized instruction packets that attempted to teach, provide practice, and test, with only minimal support from the teacher and none from fellow students. A guide should supplement instruction, not try to replace it.

Sense of Community

Finally, we come to the most important self-management tool, mentioned earlier: the development of community. Differentiated instruction is going to take students beyond rules of behavior in ways that cannot be anticipated. If we want students to work together peacefully and productively under any circumstances, we have to take the time and trouble to mold them into a community. Many books and articles have been written on this topic, so I am not going to try to describe the process (or rather, the various approaches to the process) here. Remember that every group of children is different, and with some groups there seem to be inherent incompatibilities or, worse, hostilities that have developed outside the classroom and seeped in. I do know, however, that teachers, through their own examples and their sharp eyes for good student examples, have considerable power to influence their students' attitudes and behavior, and it's worthwhile for them to exert that power to turn a group of strangers into a caring and respectful community.

Human Resources

There is one more component of the differentiated classroom that I want to discuss before leaving this topic, and that is extra adults in the classroom. When you are differentiating instruction, it is a godsend to have someone else to shush the class while you are deep in conference with one student. Many schools have aides and parent volunteers, although neither group tends to be well trained or well used. Here is another place where teacher time and effort pay off. You don't expect aides or volunteers to do your teaching for you, but you can have them lead practice activities, monitor and assist small groups working on their own, and give simple assessments. They can also answer questions, give permissions, provide supplies, and offer friendly counsel. Instruct aides and parents about how things operate in the classroom as you would teach kids, by explaining, modeling, and giving guided and monitored practice. If there are parents who aren't able to attend training sessions, it is probably best to assign them at first only to tasks such as making copies and changing bulletin boards. While working, they can observe what aides and other volunteers do, talk with you, and learn.

To facilitate the use of aides in classrooms, principals have to schedule them wisely, but that does not always happen. You should tactfully let your principal know why having the same person in your classroom every day is better than having different people. You should also request the times that an aide would be most useful to you. As with the scheduling of special classes, it helps if teachers get together first and work out agreements. The principal is much more likely to accept a schedule teachers have agreed upon than to want to settle quarrels among them.

Less commonly seen than aides are second teachers in the classroom, but some schools have figured out how to put them there. One middle school I know has three special education teachers, one for each grade, and assigns them to spend a block of time in each teacher's classroom. Although they concentrate their attention on students classified as disabled, they include other students in their groups and give help to students who ask for it. These teachers plan with the classroom teachers and share equal status. Another possible arrangement is to have two classroom teachers working together at prearranged times by dividing their classes for different levels of instruction. This allows for more homogeneity in each group. It also allows quiet individual work to go on in one classroom while active, noisy group work goes on in the other. The groups do not have to be equal in size. When two teachers work together, both benefit from the added knowledge and ideas and the sharing of planning tasks.

All of the arrangements, equipment, materials, and strategies discussed in this chapter merely set the stage for differentiated instruction, and, as I said at the beginning, none of them is a must and any one can be modified to fit a particular teacher and her students. Now we can begin to look at the differentiation in teaching strategies, grouping, student tasks, and support that make a classroom the place where all students can learn and feel good doing it.

References

CARMICHAEL, L. B. 1981. *McDonogh 15: Becoming a School.* New York: Avon Books.

GLASSER, W. 1969. *Schools Without Failure.* New York: Harper and Row.

KOHN, A. 1996. *Beyond Discipline: From Compliance to Community.* Alexandria, VA: Association for Supervision and Curriculum Development.

MARZANO, R. J. 2003. *Classroom Management That Works: Research Based Strategies for Every Teacher.* Alexandria, VA: Association for Supervision and Curriculum Development.

SERVIS, J. 1999. *Celebrating the Fourth: Ideas and Inspiration for Teachers of Grade 4.* Portsmouth, NH: Heinemann.

The Assessment-
Teaching Loop

An old popular song tells us that "Love and marriage go together like a horse and carriage. You can't have one without the other." Well, assessment and differentiated instruction go together in the same way, each one giving to and taking from the other and growing stronger through a continuing relationship. I think that the adjectives we most often hear associated with assessment–diagnostic, authentic, formative, and summative–do not do justice to the recursiveness of the assessment process and the interdependence of its components.

Purposes of Assessment

Teachers who differentiate do so because they want to provide instruction that is right for all their students. They assess to find out what students know and what they are ready to learn. Working from that foundation, they develop plans for a lesson or a unit, but they also continue assessing while teaching so they can make any adjustments needed. After teaching, they assess again, not only to see how well students have learned, but also to see how well they taught and to decide what to teach next. Apart from general planning, teachers use assessment to tell them which students need extra support and which ones are ready to manage their own learning. For differentiating teachers, putting a level or a descriptive label on a student's learning is less important than understanding it. Although they recognize the legitimacy of the school's and parents' need to know what a student has accomplished in relation to the standards and other students, their primary concern is fostering learning. Assessing and teaching, teaching and assessing, they believe, are the best means to that end.

This chapter deals with the variety and complexity of assessment to improve teaching and learning, yet I am hoping to keep it simple. My objective throughout this book is to make differentiated instruction doable for today's teachers, who already have too many demands put upon them. So, in discussing the whats, whens, and hows of classroom assessment, I will be thinking of how you can get and use information about your students without working twenty-four-hour days.

Finding out What Students Know

To begin the assessment-teaching loop, teachers need to know where students are when they come into their classrooms at the beginning of the year. The way teachers think about literacy determines the types of assessments they use and what information they look for in assessing. As many conscientious teachers do, they can assess reading, writing, speaking and listening separately, or they can view literacy as an integrated process and assess it that way. I will describe both approaches and point out some differences in the information teachers obtain.

Most teachers assess reading in the first few weeks of the school year with published or locally developed reading inventories. Using one or more assessment tools, they identify students' instructional levels and get information about their areas of difficulty. Informally, a teacher may start by giving a student material he is sure she can read, then move her up to more difficult material until she reaches the upper limits of her ability to do smooth, error-free reading. A teacher may also present a list of words, ordered by difficulty, and ask a student to decode them. Another approach is to have a student answer comprehension questions after reading a selection or retell its content in her own words. By counting the number of errors in passage and word reading and estimating the extent of comprehension in the highest-level material a student can read comfortably, a teacher is able to place her in a reading group and steer her toward books she can read independently.

Writing is usually assessed a bit later by asking the whole class to write a piece in response to a prompt. In assessing students' written work—at any grade level—teachers tend to look for complete sentences, organization of ideas, word choice, and mechanical skills. Since they are not going to place children in groups for writing or vary writing assignments on the basis of competence, teachers don't have to be concerned with differences in sophistication of ideas or expression, qualities that are very hard to quantify anyway. What teachers want to know is where the class is in the most obvious writing skills, and what they need to work on. They also want to find out who the strugglers are and what weaknesses stand out in their writing.

In most classrooms listening and speaking are assessed incidentally through observation of students engaged in daily activities. Typically, teachers take note of only unusual performances: the student who has a large and mature vocabulary, the one who speaks nonstandard English, or the one who doesn't "get" oral instructions.

While all these assessments are useful in placing students and determining the levels of materials and tasks that are generally appropriate, they don't go very far in helping teachers understand individual strengths and needs. Nor do they lead directly to differentiated instruction. Teachers who use this approach need to follow up their initial assessments with ongoing assessments that contribute more fine-grained information. Through ongoing assessment, teachers learn much more about their students and are able to make the adjustments in instruction called for.

Before describing the integrated process approach to assessment, I need to introduce some terms involved in looking at literacy this way that I will use repeatedly in succeeding chapters. They are *reception, in-processing, storage, out-processing,* and *production.* Reception is the ability to recognize the language you hear or read (more commonly known as the skills of decoding and literal comprehension). In-processing is being able to transform language into thought (constructing meaning). Storage is holding onto meaning and information over time (integrating them into memory). Out-processing is turning thought back into language (verbalizing meaning). And production is being able to organize and express meaning and information in clear, concise, and culturally appropriate speech and writing (composing with form and style). These terms and the relations between them are illustrated in Figure 3-1.

In an integrated process assessment, a student reads a short article or story and tells about it, just as he would in a separate domain assessment. But he does not have to answer questions or decode isolated words. If a student falters in retelling a story, the teacher prompts him to keep him going, so that he has the opportunity to tell everything he remembers. Then, the teacher asks the student what he thinks the piece means or what message it communicated to him. Again, the teacher may prompt to help the student

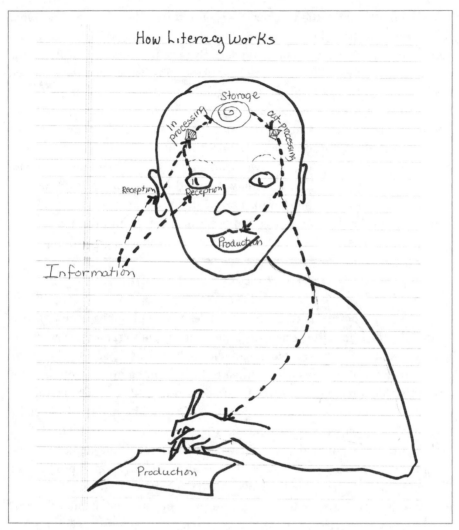

FIGURE 3-1: *How Literacy Works*

express himself more fully and accurately. Next, the student writes about the piece—its content and meaning—but first the teacher guides him in constructing an outline of what he wants to say. Throughout the assessment, the teacher continues to prompt the student and engage him in conversation about the story. Prompting does not mean telling students the correct answers, but stopping them or slowing them down when they have forgotten an important point or misstated something. So a teacher might say, "Is that all that happened?" "Tell me that again; I'm not sure I understand." "When you say the character 'freaked out,' do you mean he got frightened or angry or what?"

A day or two later, the teacher meets with the student again to see what he remembers, have him read aloud his (uncorrected) written essay, and comment on it. This second meeting not only tests memory, it also allows the student to show whether or not he has further processed the piece, refined his language, and exercised critical judgment on his own performance.

In this way, teachers not only assess reception, processing, storage, and production of oral and written language in one continuous sweep, but also see where the process may be breaking down for some students. If during an assessment, one or two components of literacy suggest weaknesses, teachers can follow up later with another assessment that focuses on the areas they want more information about. In the next section, I give three examples of how an integrated process assessment might go.

Examples of Integrated Process Assessment

After Jason smoothly read a short article on keeping tropical fish, his teacher asked him to tell what the important things to remember were. He was able to do so quite completely and accurately. But when asked to write a summary for other kids who wanted to keep fish, he mixed unimportant details with main ideas and wrote in run-on sentences. The following day he was able to remember most of the important points he had read. When he reread his own paper, however, he expressed dissatisfaction, saying, "This isn't right," and crumpled it up. His teacher concluded that Jason had good reception, processing, and storage skills, but he needed help in production. The fact that he recognized the inadequacy of his written piece was very encouraging. This was a literate boy who could operate independently most of the time. For writing, he needed to learn strategies for selecting and organizing information and editing his drafts. His teacher thought he could benefit from working with a patient and systematic partner.

When Marissa stumbled over several words on the first page of the story she was given to read, her teacher suggested that they take turns reading short sections of it. Even then Marissa couldn't complete certain sentences and gave up. Her teacher read those sentences, too. Because Marissa struggled and stopped throughout the story, her teacher reread all of it aloud afterward, and then began to discuss it with Marissa. Marissa was able to retell and interpret the story very well. She was also able to suggest a sensible outline for writing. However, when Marissa began to write her piece, she quickly became frustrated at not being able to spell many of the words. She wrote only simple, childish sentences, but they were grammatically correct and properly punctuated. The finished piece was nowhere near the quality of her retelling and had many misspelled words. The following day Marissa retold the story without prompting. She reread her own writing haltingly and had little to say about it afterward.

The teacher concluded that Marissa's reception and production of oral language were good. She also appeared to process and store information competently. Yet both reception and production of written language were seriously hampered by her lack of word analysis and synthesis skills. Marissa needed a lot of catch-up instruction in de-constructing and constructing words. Since she appeared bright and eager to learn, though embarrassed by her inadequacies, the teacher decided that very small temporary groups and extra tutoring by the teacher, an aide, or an older student were the best ways to go. Marissa might also benefit from listening to and "echo reading" taped selections before encountering them in her reading group.

Allison read a selection about television advertising quite smoothly, but beyond a literal and limited retelling she could not pick out its important points. She dictated an outline for her teacher that wasn't much better. When asked to write about her reactions to the selection, she produced a short piece that was technically correct, but had little content. She said she thought the article was good, but gave no reasons why. The following day, Allison did not remember much of what she had read. When her teacher prompted her, she would say, "Oh, yes" and then complete that piece of information, but she was not able to continue from memory. She read her own writing and indicated satisfaction with it.

Allison's teacher suspected serious problems with processing and storage. Perhaps Allison would need to be tested by a learning disability specialist later in the year, but first the teacher wanted to try some strategies. In accepting her own inadequate performance without trying to improve it, Allison also showed signs that she thought she was "dumb," and that bothered her teacher. She decided that Allison could function superficially in a mid-level reading group, and it would be better for her self-esteem to put her there than in a lower group. But, Allison also needed extra instruction and practice, particularly in paraphrasing what she read, taking notes, and rereading. Constructing categories of information after reading a text seemed to be a good practice activity for her. Sharing oral retellings with a more astute partner would be good, too. The teacher also decided to require Allison to make a detailed outline before writing and to write longer pieces than she was now doing. She would then be sure to praise her for quantity even if the quality was not up to par.

These illustrations of integrated process assessment take no more teacher time or effort than the discrete assessments described earlier, but as you can see, they yield more information for differentiating instruction at the beginning of the school year. Differentiating teachers also have to use ongoing assessments to see progress (or lack of it) and determine further changes in instruction, but they are several steps ahead of teachers who use discrete assessments for student placement and general planning of instruction.

While, obviously, I am encouraging teachers to try integrated process assessment, I recognize that using it requires the ability to do a sophisticated analysis of students' literacy on the spot. This is an ability that observant teachers develop over time as they work with hundreds of children and become aware of all the subtle messages contained in their performances. If you do not feel ready to do this complex type of assessment now, you should stick with more conventional assessments for the time being and try out a integrated process assessment on one or two students when you are not under the pressure of time. It would also be a good idea to try to analyze videotapes of students reading aloud. While watching them you will have more time to think about what you're seeing and can replay parts that are difficult to interpret.

Formal Assessments

Many writers and teachers define *formal assessment* as a published test, administered under fixed conditions and scored according to standardized norms or established criteria. I am using the term somewhat differently to denote any planned-for and structured type of assessment that is given to all students in essentially the same format. In my view teachers can develop effective formal assessments and score them in accordance with their own expectations. For example, a pretest and posttest on the content of a science unit is a formal assessment. On the other hand, an assessment that is unplanned for, varied in structure, and unscored is an informal assessment. An example of that would be a group reading activity in which the teacher has different students read aloud and then decides it would be a good time to take notes on their decoding and fluency competence. The type of integrated assessment I have described in this chapter is a mixed breed. Basically, it is a formal assessment because it is planned for and structured and given to all students in the same format. But because the inner procedures of the assessment vary as students responses vary, and because it is not scored, in that sense it is also an informal assessment.

Differentiating teachers use both formal and informal assessments. The formal assessments enable teachers to get a sense of the class as a whole, identify the general reading level of each student, make big curricular decisions, and report out to students, parents, and administrators. Informal assessments allow teachers to check on the effects of their teaching, make short-term instructional plans, and catch any signs of difficulty or advancement in their students. When I say formal assessments are planned for, I mean that they are deliberately given, scheduled at particular times, and recognized by students as assessments. A formal assessment also has an announced purpose, as when a teacher hands out a written survey on which students are to check the kinds of books they like to read, so she can order more books for the classroom library. Here are some other types of formal assessments differentiating teachers might use and their main purposes:

◆ *Student Interviews*—to find out student interests, attitudes, habits, and past experience

◆ *Parent Surveys*—to find out about students' literacy practices outside of school, parents' perceptions of their child's abilities and progress, and what home and community support for literacy learning is available

◆ *Pretest and Posttests*—to determine the level of students' knowledge before and after a unit of instruction

◆ *Checklists*—to get a quick picture of what students like and dislike, what they have done in the past; to find out which students have similar interests for possible grouping or partnering

◆ *Published Reading Inventories*—to place students in groups, get a general idea of their literacy strengths and weaknesses

◆ *Published Skills Analyses*—to identify specific weaknesses; to better understand the literacy operations of students with puzzling performances

◆ *Videotaped Performances*—to do a thorough analysis of students' oral reading; to compare with later videotaped samples for evidence of progress

All of the formal assessments above yield information for differentiating instruction, but considering how busy teachers are, I think interviews are the most economical and productive type of formal assessment. Although interview questions are set ahead of time, answers are fuller and the teacher can ask follow-up questions if he needs to know more. Published skills analyses are excellent for identifying specific problems of young readers and disabled readers, although they do not fit older, normally progressing readers. On the other side, I think checklists are the least useful form of assessment because they allow students to answer without thinking or explaining. It is too easy to follow the impulse of the moment or give the teacher what you think he wants.

Basal series often have end-of-unit and end-of-book tests that are intended to tell teachers whether students are ready to go on to the next story or book. I have not included these in my list because I think they are often unreliable determiners of reading competence, and they give very little information for differentiating. I have also not listed portfolios. They are cumulative, polished performances that may be helpful to next year's teacher, but they won't help with this year's planning or differentiation.

Informal Assessments

As I said above, informal assessments are not planned for or structured. Nevertheless, teachers have to be prepared for them. In the course of every school day students perform dozens of literacy acts that reveal important information about their learning. Everything, from spending five minutes sharpening one's pencils when it's silent reading time to explaining a task to a classmate who doesn't understand, is a student literacy performance worth noting. Although no one expects teachers to see all performances, they have to be ready for the ones that take place right before their eyes (and ears). Again, I will list types of assessments and indicate their primary purposes, but this time my list will be less comprehensive. There are just too many ways that teachers can assess informally in the context of the classroom.

◆ *Observing students at work*—to find out how well students perform any number of literacy acts under realistic conditions; to note specific problems

◆ *Asking for a retelling*—to check on accuracy and completeness of reception; to check on oral language production

◆ *Holding a conference*—to explore points of concern that have surfaced in other assessments; to identify areas of advanced literacy performance and plan for continuing progress in those areas

- ◆ *Comparing earlier to later written work*–to look for growth and repeated errors; to determine what students should work on next

- ◆ *Asking "why" and "how" questions*–to learn more about students' processing of texts

- ◆ *Asking students to repeat or paraphrase what others have said*–to check on listening reception, oral language processing, and production

- ◆ *Asking students to recall past reading*–to check on storage effectiveness

- ◆ *Asking students to summarize what they have read*–to examine organizational skills and language production

- ◆ *Asking students to explain the meaning of a phrase or a sentence*–to check on reception, processing, and language production

- ◆ *Asking students to read aloud*–to determine the level of reception; to note types of errors; to assess processing (through phrasing, intonation, and emphasis)

- ◆ *Giving multistep directions*–to check oral reception and processing of language into action

Most of these and other informal assessments can be used for purposes other than those stated. Because they are informal, they are also flexible, so that teachers can focus on whatever areas they want to find out more about. As you probably noticed, the term "processing" is used liberally in describing purposes. This is because informal assessments are very useful in helping teachers figure out what is going on with students' thinking. Since formal assessments rarely have the power to do that, differentiating teachers need to use frequent and varied informal assessments. I mentioned earlier the importance of ongoing assessment, and I would like to reemphasize that here; ongoing assessment helps you follow the growth in students' processing that is happening all the time.

Keeping Records

One thing true of all successful differentiating teachers is that they have excellent literacy skills. These teachers are able to receive, process, and store a vast quantity of oral and written language produced by their students. And they can talk and write about their students' language with clarity and detail. We often fail to notice, however, that their skills are supported by the notes and records they keep. Assessment may be spontaneous and free-wheeling, but record keeping is deliberate and exacting. How do busy teachers do it?

First, you need a system. Second, you have to have the tools of that system handy all the time. Systems vary a great deal, from checklists to notes, rating scales, or categories. In watching lots of teachers, I've gathered that the most popular system is taking notes and transcribing them onto a skills checklist later that day. Some teachers take their notes in a small notebook, others in their plan book, and still others in the margins of the books or other materials they're using. What seems to me to be the most efficient way is to write a few words on a sticky note and attach it to whatever will help you remember completely and accurately how the student performed.

When it comes to recording information, I will suggest a system that brings together what I think are the best elements of all the things I've seen teachers do. It's a set of charts with coded information about important literacy components and markers for difficulty and success. To use it the teacher makes a class set of charts with grids and the name of a student across the top of each one. Down the side are listed the specific components the student is working on, with room for new components to be added. There should also be room for comments. When an assessment is done, the teacher fills in a box next to it with the coded result and the date. The code, which represents the quality of the performance, can be anything that is easy to remember. It would be an advantage, I think, to construct a code based on an acronym that can be shared with students (and with parents). Here's one possibility suggested by the work of a teacher I admire. She regularly tells her first graders that they are "getting smart" as they work hard and learn more. Since the children seem to grow an inch every time she tells them this, I've chosen "S-M-A-R-T" as the code acronym for showing progress on the chart. Thus, to students the letters the teacher records for each skill and their meanings would be:

S = Starting out right

M = Making an effort

A = Advancing

R = Reaching for independence

T = Terrific

When students receive a "T," they know they've succeeded in that area and are ready to move on. They may read the teacher's comments and add their own, if they wish.

To the teacher the code has a somewhat different translation, but one that is not in conflict with the meanings students understand.

S = Hasn't grasped the concept yet

M = Can do it with lots of support

A = Can do it with a little support

R = Can do it, but is still shaky

T = Can operate independently

This code would also remind the teacher of the kind of support each student needs. S and M indicate that the teacher should work with the student on that skill; A suggests that an aide or trained volunteer can guide practice; R means that the student is ready to work with a partner; and T means that not only can the student work on his own, he can also help others.

Taking the system one step farther, the teacher can highlight S's and T's in color, so that when she or a student looks at the chart they can see instantly the areas still weak and those mastered. Figure 3-2 illustrates what one student's chart might look like.

When a student can operate independently in all or most of the components on a chart, a new chart should be started. By keeping and using such charts throughout the year, along with anecdotal comments, teachers have a complete and usable record of individual learning patterns to guide differentiation and report progress.

Making Time for Assessment

I think I left the question of finding time for assessment till the end because I haven't got a satisfactory answer. Informal assessments can be done while you're teaching, and ongoing formal ones, such as interviews, can be done any time you have a few minutes. But the beginning of the year assessments given to all students demand hours of quiet, uninterrupted time. Without another competent adult to take over the classroom, instruction declines, and the quality of assessment may decline, too. It used to be that schools would hire substitutes for a few days so teachers

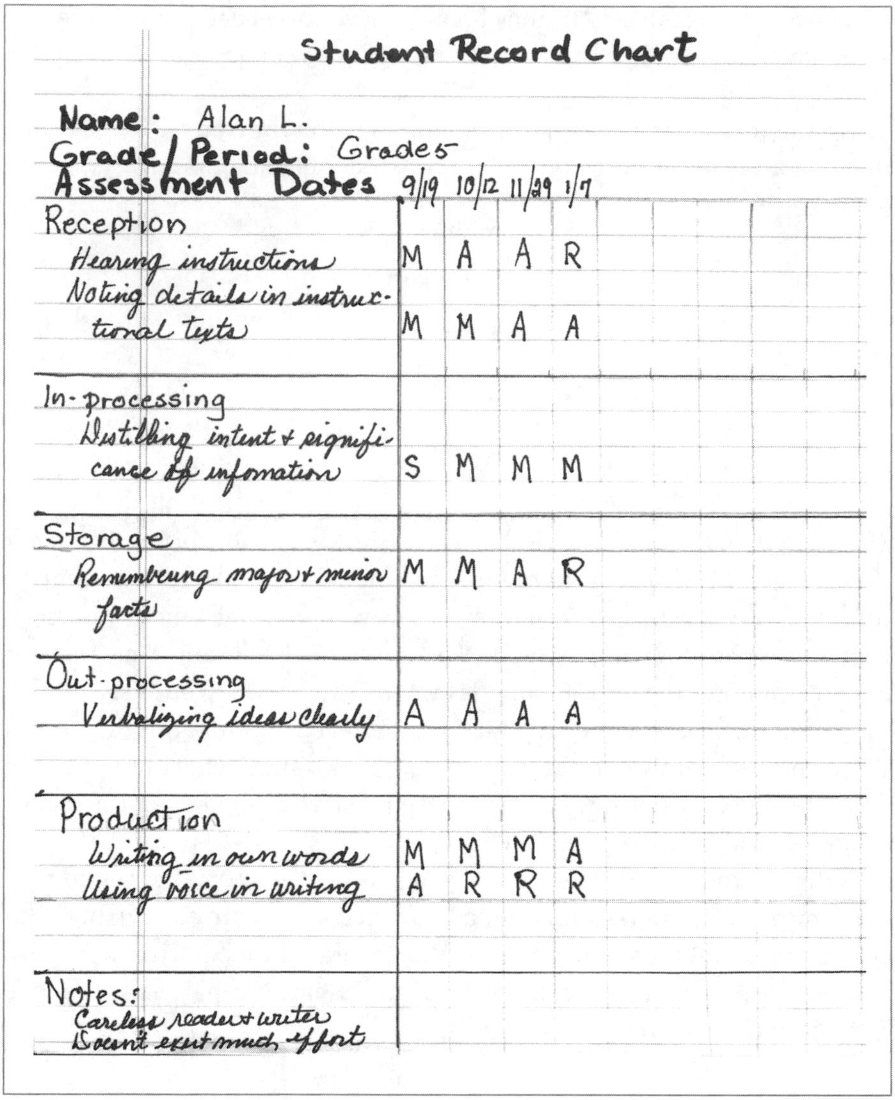

Student Record Chart

Name: Alan L.
Grade/Period: Grade 5
Assessment Dates: 9/19 10/12 11/29 1/7

	9/19	10/12	11/29	1/7
Reception				
Hearing instructions	M	A	A	R
Noting details in instructional texts	M	M	A	A
In-processing				
Distilling intent & significance of information	S	M	M	M
Storage				
Remembering major & minor facts	M	M	A	R
Out-processing				
Verbalizing ideas clearly	A	A	A	A
Production				
Writing in own words	M	M	M	A
Using voice in writing	A	R	R	R

Notes:
Careless reader & writer
Doesn't exert much effort

FIGURE 3-2: *Student Record Chart*

could do their beginning of the year assessments, or they'd have kids come in one at a time before classes were in session. Since I don't see either of those things happening again any time soon, what can you do to make time for assessment?

One possible solution is to use a week's worth of literacy blocks for assessments, while an aide or volunteer oversees the class doing work that doesn't require a teacher. To provide a little more time, some parents might be willing to bring their children in before school or let them stay after school for assessment. A colleague might also be persuaded to combine your class with hers for a large-group activity. If none of these plans is possible, you will have to borrow time from wherever you can find it. Think about starting the day with an extra thirty minutes of silent reading; inviting an older student or a parent to lead the morning routines and read a story aloud; sending the class out to the playground with a parent for a long recess; showing a video at the end of the day (connected to the current science or social studies unit, I hope); or giving up your planning periods to supervise a colleague's class while she assesses and ask her to do the same for you. Although I've known teachers to do all of the above, the most common practice is to bribe the class to work quietly for thirty to forty minutes at a time with the promise of a party or an extra recess at the end of the week. One way or another, teachers overcome the odds and get their assessments done.

The Importance of Assessment

The willingness of differentiating teachers to create their own assessments, give up their professional and personal time, and keep detailed records of student learning is testimony to their belief in the importance of assessment. What they know is that you can't just follow the textbook, hand out worksheets, or create a bunch of "fun" lessons and expect all students to thrive. Students learn when the instruction is right for them. And instruction is right when it is based on sensitive, thorough, and ongoing assessment.

References

BARR, M.A., ET AL., eds. 1999. *Assessing Literacy with the Learning Record: A Handbook for Teachers.* Portsmouth, NH: Heinemann.

BEAVER, JOETTA. 1997. *Developmental Reading Assessment.* Glenview, IL: Celebration Press.

JOHNS, J. L. 1997. *Basic Reading Inventory: Pre-Primer through Grade Twelve and Early Literacy Assessments.* Dubuque, IA: Kendall/Hunt.

JOHNSTON, P. 1997. *Knowing Literacy: Constructive Literacy Assessment.* York, ME: Stenhouse.

LEWIN, L., AND B. J. SHOEMAKER. 1998. *Great Performances: Creating Classroom-Based Assessment Tasks.* Alexandria, VA: Association for Supervision and Curriculum Development.

Grouping and Teaching for Foundational Literacy

Teachers have always had expectations for what their students should learn. In the first half of the twentieth century expectations grew out of school traditions, personal experience, and the demands of the instructional materials teachers were given to use. From the 1960s through the '90s, however, as language arts textbooks yielded to collections of fiction and nonfiction books, reference materials, videotapes, and the Internet, many teachers altered their expectations, basing them more on their informed understanding of where students were in their learning than on tradition or textbooks. Consequently, expectations differed from teacher to teacher, from school to school, and even from one year to another for the same teacher. Now, with the advent of the standards movement the situation has changed again. Not only has the movement made expectations uniform and explicit within each state, but it has also stretched many expectations to fit the notions of competence held by politicians and special interest groups. In addition, it has changed the meaning of the word *expectations* from "what we hope will happen" to "what will happen, or else." As a result, many teachers find themselves caught between what they believe is best for their students as individuals and what the state says is mandatory for all, regardless of ability or circumstances.

The position of this book is that teachers can serve both their students and the standards through differentiated instruction. The fact that we are dealing with literacy is a plus because literacy opens up more possibilities for differentiated teaching and integrated learning than other disciplines. By helping individual students to reach their own highest levels of competence and challenge within the domain of literacy skills and knowledge, teachers can ensure that all their students attain foundational literacy.

What Is Foundational Literacy?

Foundational literacy is a slippery term that changes its shape with the demands of each situation. People working in offices, stores, and factories today certainly need to be more literate than their parents who held similar jobs. For students in today's standards-based classrooms the bar has also been raised. Students of any age need to be able to read, write, and speak well enough to learn the content expected in their classrooms, to interact productively within their families, to communicate clearly with adults, and to play the roles expected of them in their communities. Stated more succinctly, foundational literacy is the ability to participate effectively in language activities within the various groups in which one is a member on a regular basis.

In conventional classrooms, where everyone uses the same textbooks and does the same assignments, students who are struggling with literacy will find some reading, writing, and speaking activities difficult, if not absolutely beyond their reach, and their inadequacies may carry over to some of the other contexts in which they operate. In differentiated classrooms where teachers support struggling students with personalized instruction and appropriate materials and tasks, foundational literacy is within the reach of all students and applicable to real-world situations. Although struggling students and their more accomplished classmates may be aware of the differences in their levels of competence, those differences are not an impediment to their working and learning together.

Nevertheless, a caveat is in order. In any mixed-ability classroom, some students who are making good progress will still be below what is considered "grade level" at the end of the year. Contrary to the popular belief that children not reading on grade level by grade three will always be poor readers, many students catch up with their peers in later grades. In addition, there are students who produce high-quality work in classroom activities but fall apart under the demands of formal testing. In the rural, high-poverty school where I was principal for twelve years, we consistently saw almost all our students scoring at grade level or above by the end of eighth grade, even though a quarter to a third of them had tested below grade level in third grade.

Although the structures and strategies of differentiation discussed in this chapter will help slow-progressing students make significant growth and will bolster the independence of the test-shy, they cannot work the magic to ensure that all will pass "the test" at the designated time.

Determining the Skills and Knowledge of Foundational Literacy

Understandably, teachers want to know which skills and knowledge they have to teach for their students to attain foundational literacy. But literacy doesn't work in a prescribed, discrete, and linear way. Although literacy involves a host of skills, the same skills are practiced continually from the primary grades on and used in concert most of the time. The skills high school seniors use in writing their literary critiques or research papers are the same ones kindergartners use when they listen to stories or talk about the growth of tadpoles. In addition, the skills of any individual student do not all grow at the same rate. For example, production of language (speech and writing) is usually slower to mature than reception (literal understanding).

The essential knowledge content of literacy is really very small. For the most part, such knowledge is the common forms and conventions of written language, such as capitalization, spelling, and punctuation, and the typical structures, plot patterns, and devices found in different kinds of literature and nonfiction. While the body of mechanical writing conventions is fixed, there is no agreed-upon collection or sequence of books, stories, plays, and poems that students must read in school. Teachers who know literature select from the hundreds of fine pieces of the past and present, and offer choices they believe are appropriate for their students.

For these reasons it is more fruitful for differentiating teachers to think about literacy skills and knowledge growing outward in all directions from a core than to try to construct a traditional scope and sequence. As I said in the previous chapter, everything people do with language (the use of literacy skills and knowledge), can fit under the terms *reception*, *in-processing*, *storage*, *out-processing*, and *production*. We receive language by hearing or reading it, and we translate words and phrases into meaning in our heads. We store some of that meaning—and often specific words—in memory, turn meaning back into language, and organize language into spoken or written structures. This process is not a sequence; all five operations go on simultaneously and are recursive as well. Thus, at any grade level we want students to be able to receive, in-process, store, out-process, and produce language appropriate to their own development and experience and adequate to the demands of the materials and tasks they are given in school and the roles they play outside school. As school subject matter increases in quantity and becomes more dense with ideas and information, we want students' skills and knowledge to grow and become more integrated to accommodate the greater load.

I will try to suggest the nature of literacy growth in a diagram (Figure 4-1) by putting in a few skills that are typical of children's competence when they begin kindergarten and twelve years later when they graduate from high school. But you must understand that the skills named and even the shape of the diagram are theoretical generalizations, not realities. Our literacy competencies do expand, deepen, and become more precise, but they do not grow evenly or in a straight line. For example, although linguists have shown through research that infants' language production starts with single words (usually nouns) and proceeds from there to two-word sentences

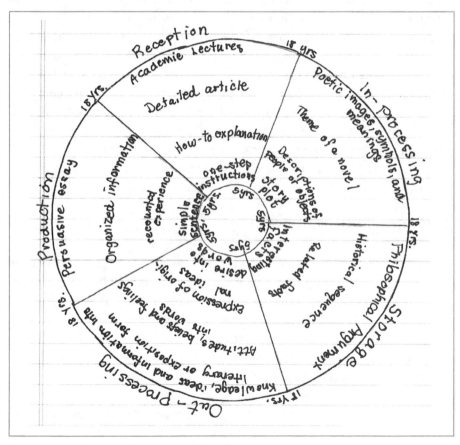

FIGURE 4-1: *Literacy Development Circle*

(noun and verb), they do not claim that sentences continue growing by adding words or that infants' reception replicates the pattern of production. Thus, it is very difficult to use words, which are discrete, and diagrams, which are finite, to illustrate components that are neither finite nor discrete and a process that never stands still or reaches a finished state.

This long and theoretical discussion of literacy development was necessary as an introduction to differentiated instruction for foundational literacy. It explains why I am not going to follow the popular conception of a linear skills curriculum or list differentiated activities on a grade-by-grade basis. Instead, I will direct my attention to the five components of literacy and activities that foster their growth. It also explains why I will assert that half the business of differentiating instruction is managing the demands of the materials and the tasks presented to students, and that the other half is giving each student the support he needs to use those materials and tasks to make continuous improvement.

From this point on let us talk about the particulars of differentiation in relation to foundational literacy. Assessment is the first step. Using ongoing assessments, discussed in the previous chapter, teachers can determine the particular literacy levels and needs of their students and build the curriculum around them. This does not mean creating a different curriculum for each student, but developing an umbrella curriculum in which every student can find a place, then forming small, flexible groups of students with similar needs and teaching to those groups. Various components of the literacy umbrella curriculum will be described in future chapters; here I will discuss only grouping and differentiated activities.

Grouping for Differentiation

Within a mixed-ability classroom there are three types of grouping needed for differentiation: long-term groups, based on similar levels of accomplishment; temporary groups, based on shared needs or interests; and virtual groups, also based on shared needs, but existing only in the teacher's planning. Formal and informal assessments, done periodically, will help teachers determine long-term groups for reading. Observations of day-to-day student performances and interests will guide the teacher in forming temporary groups and virtual groups.

Almost all teachers divide their classes into reading groups, but those groups often do not work as well as they should. In many ways, conventional reading groups fall short on differentiation. The most common problem in an ability-organized group is the differences in pace among readers. Some students don't want to put a book down once they've started it. Others are content to take it in small bites, attending to other interests in their free time. Then the faster readers, frustrated with the pace of the group, may snipe at their slower classmates, resist assignments that seem to slow down things even more, or give away the ending of the book before others have finished it. One technique many teachers use to handle this problem is to have all students reading two books at the same time, one for group instruction and one for personal reading. Students have free choice of the second book and may read it as fast as they want to, but they are asked to read the first book at the pace of the group. The thirst for reading being what it is, not everyone sticks to the rules about the group book, but no one dares complain and no one seems bored.

Another problem with ability grouping is that some students do not want to be in the group where they have been placed. Maybe one or two think they are better readers than the rest of the group. Another student is uncomfortable with a couple of group members who seem to be snickering at her when she makes a mistake. At the root of this problem is the permanency of ability-based reading groups. Teachers decide who goes where at the beginning of the year, and that's where they stay. Groups can remain constant for years if they are locked into a commercial reading system that says all students must cover all books in the series. So although this kind of grouping pays lip service to differentiated instruction, it is really its antithesis. Teachers who are serious about differentiation assess students continually and move them to other groups when there are good reasons to do so. They also reconstitute groups periodically to give everyone a fresh start. If the relative reading levels of most students do not change enough to justify total group reconstitution, teachers can still do it once in a while on the basis of students' desires to read certain books. In the intermediate and middle school grades, the time to consider making changes in groups is when students have finished a particular book or topical unit. In primary grades, I suggest every four to six weeks. Time enough for children to need a change.

A teacher problem is having too many reading groups to handle. With five or six groups in a classroom, meetings are shorter and less frequent than they should be, and some students are neglected. This problem is harder to solve than the others because teachers who over-group take small differences in students' reading competence more seriously than they should and feel duty-bound to differentiate for them. They forget that many students can operate above their independent reading level with support and that fast-moving students can benefit from operating slightly below their level if their books are interesting, the tasks are challenging, and the pace of the group is lively. My advice to any teacher is not to have more than four reading groups. Even with a class of thirty, four groups will allow you to place six students in each of the two groups that need a lot of support, and nine students in the two more independent groups. With a smaller class—twenty-four or less—three groups can cover all students' needs and let you have some breathing room.

Still another and more troubling problem for teachers is what to do with outliers. In any classroom there are always a couple of kids at either end of the spectrum who don't fit into any group. Please resist the temptation to individualize their reading programs. Although outliers do need extra attention, they also need to be part of a group, and they can be helped to blend in. Struggling readers can keep pace with their group by doing echo reading along with an audiotape. They can also benefit from reading alternate sections of an assignment with a partner. Both these types of assisted reading have been proven to improve readers' skills. And knowing that they do not have do all the work on their own improves students' attitudes toward reading. If the teacher knows that the next group meeting will involve oral reading or finding specific passages in the text, she can help a struggling reader to succeed by giving her the chance to prepare ahead of time. In the following vignette, a mixed-ability group is meeting with their teacher. Jon is a slow-progressing student who has listened to most of the group book on tape, while Milton and Helen are advanced readers.

Advanced readers make good tutors for younger children and good audiotapers for their struggling classmates. In one first-grade classroom I know, two fifth graders regularly lead a reading group and follow the teacher's "lesson plan." Their teaching consists of guiding practice on what the teacher has already taught, but it gives the first graders the extra time and attention they need. Advanced readers also need to be able to move outward and ahead, exploring other works by authors they like, trying more difficult books, new genres, and the classics. That's where personal reading comes in. While waiting for others in the group to catch up in the group book, a fast reader can devour two or three personal books on his own.

Temporary groups are not a common feature in today's classrooms, yet they are an accommodation sorely needed by students who are slow in attaining foundational literacy. The trouble is not that teachers don't see that some of their students need extra help, but that they don't know how to fit it in. Where do you find the time? And what do the other kids do while you're teaching a temporary group? The simplest answer is to pull a group together when the rest of the class is working on a language task that includes the skill you want to teach. For example, while the class is working

An Intermediate Reading Group Meets

For about a week, one of Marlys Sloup's reading groups has been reading *From the Mixed up Files of Mrs. Basil E. Frankweiler,* by E. L. Konigsburg. In the story, two runaway children hide in New York City's Metropolitan Museum of Art and solve a mystery surrounding a renaissance statue. The book is notable not only for its sophisticated plot and wealth of information about museums but also for its rich portrayal of character. This week, as she meets the group twice for discussion, Ms. Sloup is focusing on the personalities of the two children. Her sole question today is, "What are Jamie and Claudia like?" She asks students to identify the children's characteristics and to refer to places in the story where those characteristics are brought out. They may read short sections aloud to prove their points.

The children start with Claudia, who, after all, is the main character. Quickly, various children mention that she is "smart," "elegant," "fussy," "selfish," "likes comfort," "is a good planner." As they say the words, Ms. Sloup writes them on a piece of paper without comment. When they have exhausted their suggestions, she reads the whole list aloud and then picks out one word.

Ms. S.: *Debbie, you said "fussy"; why do you think so?*
Debbie: *Well, she made Jamie change his underwear every day, and they had to take baths on Saturday.*
Jon: *I don't think that makes her fussy. You change your underwear and take baths, don't you? (Everyone giggles.)*
Debbie: *Yeah, but I wouldn't if I ran away. I'd be like Jamie.*
Ms. S.: *What is his attitude?*
Debbie: *(Searching for the page in the book.) Wait a minute, Here, on page 80, Claudia says, "I really can't stand one night more without a bath," and Jamie says, "I don't mind."*

(Jon remains quiet; he seems convinced.)

Ms. S.: *Any other evidence?*
Milton: *How about her eating only breakfast food for breakfast?*

Kim: *But she changed her mind when she got hungry.*
Milton: *That still doesn't change it; she was fussy about food.*
Helen: *And she's always correcting Jamie's grammar.*

After a few more comments, the group seems satisfied that Claudia is indeed fussy. Ms. Sloup moves on.

Ms. S.: *I'm interested in your choice of "selfish," Paul. Where in the story do you find her being selfish?*
Paul: *Well, wanting to take a taxi all the time when they didn't have much money.*
Kim: *That wasn't selfish; she just liked to be comfortable.*
Paul: *Well, how about when she kept Jamie and Ms. Frankweiler waiting for lunch while she took a bath?*
Debbie: *She didn't realize they were waiting.*
Milton: *I think Paul is right. The big thing is that she didn't care that her parents were worrying about them. It was selfish to run away in the first place. She didn't have it so bad.*
Jon: *But she didn't know they were worrying either. She didn't think about that.*
Ms. S.: *Both Debbie and Jon have made the point that Claudia didn't "realize" or didn't "think" about what others were feeling. Does that mean she was selfish?*
Helen: *No.*
Milton: *Yes. She found time to think about what she cared about, like hot fudge sundaes.*
Helen: *But she wasn't selfish about the Michelangelo sketch. She wanted Ms. Frankweiler to give it to the museum.*

The argument goes on for several minutes with all the children chiming in. No consensus is reached.

Ms. S.: *I don't think we're going to agree on whether or not Claudia was selfish right now. Maybe some of you will change your minds when you finish the book. Think about it as you read. Look up* selfish *in the dictionary, and get a precise definition. See if it fits Claudia. Now, let's go on to Jamie. What was he like?*

on editing papers they've written, you can gather a few students who are weak in editing skills and walk them through the editing process using a sample paper on an overhead projector. Or you can have a small group compose a group summary of an article the class has read while everyone else is writing individual summaries. In the following vignette, a teacher works with a temporary group that needs practice in decoding and other word identification skills.

Word Card Games for Reading

"Busy Bees meet with me in the little room." announces Cindy Gleason, one member of a two-teacher team in the kindergarten. Eight children scramble to find their word card envelopes in their personal storage bins, then follow her to the room just off the kindergarten. While they are working together here, the other kindergarten teacher will supervise the rest of the two classes in a combined activity period.

The word cards have been collected over time as the children dictate stories, read signs and special words around the room, write their own names, and learn about science and social studies topics. Having a card does not mean that a child can read the word, only that he or she was interested enough to ask for it, so the teacher wrote it out.

Ms. Gleason sits down in front of a small portable chalkboard, while the children arrange themselves in a widely spaced semicircle on the rug and unpack their word cards for the games to come. Since the group is of mixed ability—and mixed interest in reading—some children have as few as a dozen cards while others have as many as fifty. They spread out several cards around themselves; of course, those who have large packs cannot use them all at one time.

"Let's start with the longest word you have," suggests Ms. Gleason, to begin a game of word and sound sensitivity that does not demand actual reading. The children hunt for their longest word, sometimes comparing a few cards to make sure they have chosen correctly. Gina holds up *rabbit;* Tim chooses *computer.* There is variety in both the length and topic orientation of the words chosen.

The teacher looks around the circle to approve each word individually. If the children can read their words, that's fine. If not, the teacher reads them aloud. Then she proposes another task, "Find a word with a double letter," and a third, "Find a word that starts with the same letter as your name." Each time she checks and praises choices, and reads (or has the child read) the word aloud.

The next set of games requires some reading skill from the children. Ms. Gleason asks all those who have cards naming animals to hold them up. She asks for people words such as *boy* and *Dad.* She asks for words about spring and then words about homes, the class's latest topic of study. When children do not hold up a card, she will help them find one in the pack or ask if they would like to have one. If so, she writes the requested word on a blank card and gives it to the child.

Finally, the children use their cards to make sentences. Since most of the words in their packs are nouns, Ms. Gleason supplies pronouns and verbs by starting a sentence on her chalkboard: "I saw" or "I like to play with." She does not mention connecting words and articles, but allows children to discover their absence: "I need 'and,'" says Marcie. "May I have a 'the'?" asks Matthew. Next time, they will have greater versatility in their packs because of the added words.

After the games are over, the children copy one or more of the sentences they made into their language notebooks and put all their cards back into their envelopes.

Here are some other possibilities:

> Give a shorter form of a task to the students in the group you want to work with. While others are completing the longer form, you can pull the group together for instruction.

> Schedule personal reading time (reading workshop) every day and have a temporary group meet during part of that time.

> Schedule forty-five minutes of "Temp Group" time for everyone twice a week. Form some groups by interest and others by specific need. Work with the needy groups for twenty minutes each.

In these examples, along with explaining how you can find extra time in the busy school day, I am suggesting that it's a bad idea to give slow-progressing students extra homework or keep them in at recess for extra instruction. That's punishment, and punishment mitigates against learning.

Virtual groups, as I said earlier, exist only in the teacher's planning. They are composed of students who are weak in the same skills or knowledge but who are capable of working on those things alone or with stronger students as partners. Since bringing them together as a group isn't necessary, teachers plan tasks for them that are a modified version of what other students are doing and assign those tasks during whole-class work time.

Giving Extra Support

Grouping provides a structure for differentiating for all students, but in considering foundational literacy as we are in this chapter, our focus is on giving extra support to students who haven't been able to master the foundational literacy as easily as their classmates. Let's look briefly at how groups can be used to give slow-progressing students what they need.

One thing these learners need more of is time, for all the language processes to operate. Both personality and learning style are factors that make more time necessary. I believe that lower-achieving long-term groups should meet more often and for longer periods of time than higher-achieving groups. In concrete terms this means that a classroom of thirty with four reading groups could be scheduled as in the chart in Figure 4-2. The two lower groups would meet every day, four times a week with the teacher and once with a classroom aide, student tutor, or parent volunteer. The two higher groups would meet four times a week, three times with the teacher and once with a tutor or on their own. To save you doing the arithmetic, I will

	Mon.	Tues.	Wed.	Thurs.	Fri.
High Group 1. 100 min.	30 Tchr.		25 Tchr.	20 Tchr.	25 Aide
High Group 2. 100 min.	25 Aide	30 Tchr.	25 Tchr.		20 Tchr.
Low Group 1. 140 min	25 Tchr.	25 Aide	30 Tchr.	30 Tchr.	30 Tchr.
Low Group 2. 140 min	25 Tchr.	30 Tchr.	25 Aide	30 Tchr.	30 Tchr.
Tchr. Time	80	60	80	80	80

Long Term Reading Groups Weekly Schedule

FIGURE 4-2: *Long-Term Reading Groups Weekly Schedule*

tell you that this works out to 140 minutes of instruction per week for the two lower groups and 100 minutes for the two higher groups.

This is only one of several possible schedules. It is based on having a ninety-minute literacy block with five-minute breaks in between group sessions. If a class has only three groups the meeting times can be longer. If the most needy students are all in one group, then the second-lowest group would have to meet only four times a week. Generally speaking, the need for meeting frequency decreases and for longer sessions increases as students move up through the grades. By third grade, higher-achieving groups should do just fine on three meetings per week.

Temporary groups do not normally operate on a fixed schedule. The plan of having a regular "Temp Group" time, as described earlier, is appropriate for a class where most of the students are behind in foundational skills or for a class so advanced that they want to pursue special interests pretty much on their own. With a typical class, temporary groups are formed as needed and dissolved after one or two meetings. Ideally, a group session should not last more than twenty minutes, since students are being taken away from other work that they can also benefit from and might prefer doing.

Virtual groups need either more time to complete ordinary class assignments or shorter assignments. If you are using large blocks of time flexibly for a variety of literacy activities, students in a virtual group can usually find the extra minutes to finish their work. When there are two literacy blocks a day—even if one is shorter—the teacher can use one for temporary groups or conferences with individuals, while most of the students continue writing, reading, or working on projects. In classrooms where I have seen two blocks operating, there is still ample time for other subjects, recesses, and special classes.

By allotting more time for lower long-term groups, teachers can go more slowly with presentations and practice. I am not one who believes that slow-progressing students require a different type of instruction. From my experience in classrooms I am convinced that they just need more time and more personal attention. Many such learners get overwhelmed by the flood of information coming at them in a regular full-class lesson. They panic and then shut down. In the more leisurely context of a long-term group, the teacher can present concepts slowly and have students show they understand by paraphrasing or demonstrating what she has explained. If necessary, presentations can be repeated. The group is small enough for all students to ask questions and show what they can do. It is also small enough for everyone to read aloud and retell what was read.

Teacher modeling is an essential part of supporting slow-progressing students. Typically, these students have trouble with processing what they read, but we can't see into their heads to find out what is going wrong. By modeling their own thinking as they read and write, teachers can show students how effective processing works. Teachers should model regularly for slow-progressing students, and periodically ask them to model their own thinking, too.

These students also need to practice what has been taught under the eye of the teacher. At first, such practice should be a walk-through, with the teacher coaching all along the way. Then, students can practice by themselves with the teacher monitoring to keep them on track. Finally, they should be ready to go off and work alone. But for these students who may get confused or forget, it is a good idea to write down or draw the steps in a process, so they can use them as a reminder when they work independently.

Another common need of slow-progressing students is to have a language process scaled down for them so they can focus on the parts that are most important without having to do everything. One very simple way is for the teacher to read a story aloud and then have everyone discuss it informally. (No questions to answer.) This allow students to concentrate on processing, rather than reception. The teacher can also read alternate sections of a story and ask students to read the ones she skips. This last procedure, often called interactive reading, works with group writing, too. I will describe in detail one scaled-down language activity for long-term groups in intermediate grades. It involves little or no writing, but still requires students to receive, process, store, and produce language:

1. The teacher assigns a chapter to be read and matches each student with a character whose actions and thoughts they should pay special attention to. (More than one student may be matched to a character.)

2. Students read the chapter twice, the second time giving special attention to their character and taking notes if they wish.

3. Students are asked to dramatize the chapter (without scripts), performing actions and narrating bridges between them. (If there are three characters in the chosen chapter and six students in the group, this allows two dramatizations, which stimulates better reception and production than having just one.)

As you can see, there are differences between what students do in a long-term group and in a temporary group. I'd say that long-term groups are the place for working on the major literacy processes of reception, in-processing, storage, out-processing and production, and that temporary groups are the place for discrete skills such as spelling conventions and alphabetizing. Temporary groups are also where the teacher can go over material presented to the whole class when she senses that some students haven't grasped it. Obviously, long-term groups give the teacher more time to teach complex work; but they also give students a sense of connectedness to the subject matter and the other group members. For at least some slow-progressing learners, these are strong psychological needs. They don't feel confident academically or socially in whole-class situations.

Before we move on, I want to reemphasize the role of partners in giving slow progressing learners extra attention. A partner is someone you read with and write with, not a tutor. When teachers organize students into partnerships, they should try to pair slower learners with classmates who are only moderately competent. You want someone who will not only have the patience to go more slowly, but also who will not take over and do all the work. When partners are more evenly matched, help flows in both directions. Let's look at another vignette, this time one of two partners working together on a science observation.

Keeping a Science Log

Ten days ago the third graders in Lois Peterson's class filled four small terrariums with soil and planted them with clover seeds. They kept the soil moist and made sure that the terrariums got sunlight. Now, the plants are well-sprouted and it is time to add grasshoppers, between fifteen and twenty to each terrarium. The children are excited watching the lively insects move around their new homes, but after a while they drift back to their seats and regular classwork.

Mrs. Peterson has organized the children into pairs and set up an observation schedule of five-minute periods every half hour for the next several days. That way each pair will make a formal observation every day, though children may certainly watch at other times if they are free. The formal observations will be written in a log with careful attention to completeness and exact words.

The class has brainstormed the kinds of things they want to look for: the condition of the soil and the plants; the behavior of the insects; any changes from the day before.

The next day Whitney and Lauren approach the terrarium for their turn to observe, each with a pad and pencil for taking notes. They whisper as if their voices might disturb the grasshoppers. At the end of five minutes they go to a work corner to talk and write down what they saw. Since Whitney is the more fluent writer, she volunteers to be the scribe while Lauren reads from both sets of notes. First, she puts down the date—Oct. 20—and the time—2:00 p.m. P.m.? Yes.

They talk about the poor condition of the clover plants. They both feel that the grasshoppers look much the same as when they were put in. Whitney writes:

> The soil is damp.
> The plants are droopy and lying down. Most of the leaves are gone. They look like they have been chewed.
> The grasshoppers are moving around and on the plants.
> They look healthy.
> Our conclusion—The grasshoppers are eating the plants.

By the following day, the plants are almost gone, and the groups agree that the grasshoppers are eating the plants, but the children are not sure where the grasshoppers are getting moisture from. Ms. Peterson puts some chameleons into two of the terrariums with the grasshoppers, and leaves the other two as they were. "What do you think will happen now?" she asks. The children have lots of ideas.

Differentiating Materials and Tasks

Along with extra time and more personalized instruction, slow-progressing students need differentiated materials and tasks. Although the teacher and partners can support them through difficult material in a group structure, for independent work they need materials that are at their reading level and assignments they can process and produce. The lower-grade basals, mentioned in Chapter 2 as part of a differentiated classroom library, are for personal reading, assessment, and some types of practice. For many reasons, they should not be the instructional mainstay for slow-progressing readers. In the first place, it is likely that these students have been through them already in a lower grade. They know the stories, and they don't need to be reminded that their reading is below the level of their classmates. Second, the content of the selections in these basals is usually childish, even for the grade level intended. Don't insult the intelligence of intermediate-grade students with "Dick and Jane"–type characters and their slight adventures. Third, and most important, other students will see what they are reading and recognize them as "baby books." When teachers are working so hard to create a community of equals, they should not allow this kind of divisiveness to destroy it.

Then what should teachers use? The same kinds of materials they use for faster groups: interesting fiction and nonfiction books, newspaper and magazine articles, and stories—but at a lower instructional level. At times they may also use short selections from grade-level social studies or science textbooks and reference books such as an almanac or dictionary, because slow-progressing students need to learn how to cope with them well enough to do whole-class assignments, even though they may not comprehend their contents fully.

When easier materials are used in long-term groups teachers don't have to worry about differentiating the type or quantity of tasks. Most of the time they can assign a chapter to be read or a response to be written just as they would with a faster-progressing group. They shouldn't shy away from inference or "cause and effect" questions either. The more modest demands of the material itself will accommodate the students' lesser competence. Remember, it is the students' literacy, not their intelligence, that is lagging.

Fortunately, much of classroom writing takes care of itself, too. Students will differentiate their own personal narratives, opinion pieces, and diaries of fictional characters in accordance with their abilities and personalities. If the prompts are inviting, they will give them their all. I mention prompts because I have observed too many classrooms where writing workshops were completely free-form and the results were dismal. Many students' personal journal entries, for example, tend to be a dull recitation of daily rituals. They would be much better if teachers prompted students by suggesting that they include "something mean (or silly or creative or kind) I did or saw someone else do" or "a description of the most interesting person I talked to yesterday."

Where teachers have to be more concerned with the logistics of differentiating tasks is in whole-class assignments where a particular type of form or content is expected. I am thinking of a geography report, a business letter, a review of a personal book, or a poem. With these kinds of tasks, all students need to see models and discuss what went into them and how, but slower-progressing students need simpler models, guided analysis, and perhaps some step-by-step directions. This is the kind of instruction a teacher could give in a temporary group while others are working. In addition, the teacher's expectations for production could be modified so that slower students are working on a shorter, simpler form of the class assignment.

I am going to describe two specific differentiated activities for slow-progressing learners here that I think are powerful and adaptable to almost any whole-class activity. One is called "Read, Talk, and Write." It can be used to help students working with grade-level textbooks or other informational material. It involves reception, processing, storage, and production of language.

1. The teacher assigns a short chapter or an article to be read. She has broken it into short segments that take about two minutes each to read.

2. Students of similar (or slightly different) abilities work in pairs. Using a timer, each reads silently for two minutes.

Read, Talk + Write

3. Each partner, in turn, tells the other what they have just read.

4. Both students write down the information they think is important.

5. They repeat the process until they have finished the assigned piece.

6. Partners read each other their notes.

7. Each writes a summary of the whole piece.

The second activity is called "Using Writing Frames." It guides students who have difficulty developing and organizing ideas through the structuring of a particular form of writing. In the primary grades a few short frames will do for all kinds of writing. In later grades, the teacher will probably have to construct a form to match the writing assignment. Like the first activity, using a frame involves reception, in-processing, storage, out-processing, and production. See frame on page 62 for a book review suitable for primary-grade children.

Teaching Organizational Skills

In working with slow-progressing students over time, I have come to believe that much of their difficulty with learning stems from personal disorganization. All too often such students misplace their books, lose their pencils, forget to write down their assignments, or leave their homework at home. By the time they get started on a piece of work, other students have it almost finished. When all their classmates seem so knowing and so far ahead, it is no wonder that so many slow-progressing students get discouraged and give up on school learning.

(Title of book) was fun to read. I liked _____

_____ .

(Tell why) _____

_____ .

I also liked _____ .

(Tell why) _____

_____ .

The author, (his/her name), did a good job of _____

_____ .

(Tell how) _____

_____ .

I recommend this book to _____ .

because (Summarize the points you made above) _____

_____

_____ .

Steps

1. The teacher models by writing a piece that fits the frame. She shows students that you don't have to use the exact words of the frame.

2. Students discuss other ways of filling the blanks.

3. Students use the frame to write their own pieces.

4. Students and teacher share and discuss the resulting pieces in a temporary group.

5. The next time a similar assignment is given, the teacher reviews the frame and asks students to try to vary it and expand its parts.

I believe that teachers can make a big difference in the lives of these students by teaching organizational skills along with literacy. Part of that teaching is suggesting devices that will do what distracted minds can't manage and showing students how to use them: spiral notebooks secured in a ring binder, an assignment book, a calendar with space to mark off due dates, tests, and events, a daily task list, and so on. Unfortunately, many of the students I am talking about are going to lose those devices, too, or quickly get them muddled up, and there is no easy remedy for those problems. You—with the help of parents—just have to keep reorganizing them.

The other part of teaching organizational skills is showing students a process they can use for schoolwork (one, incidentally, that works pretty well in other areas of their lives, too). That process requires a storage space or spaces, such as the devices just mentioned. When a student receives new information, in the form of handouts, a lecture, directions, definitions, an explanation, etc., she has to make a series of decisions and actions that go something like this:

1. Sort material into two groups: "I need" and "I don't need." Discard the second group.

2. Make categories for the "I need" group, such as homework assignments, unit notes, writing tips, and put information into each category. If something doesn't fit into any category, consider making a new category or discarding it.

3. Prioritize the items in each category by importance, urgency, or difficulty, etc. Consider discarding the lowest priorities.

4. Check categories regularly and work down the priorities.

I wish I could tell you that this process is foolproof, but it isn't. Your disorganized students may have trouble at every step. Typically, they will discard too many things at the beginning of the process rather than taking the trouble to sort them. And they will not only find it difficult to make decisions, but will also fail to 8act on their decisions. For example, they will categorize the material you give them, and then stuff it all into the same folder. For these reasons you will have to model the process repeatedly and walk them through it—repeatedly. You will also have to be very careful about not overwhelming their limited organizing abilities by giving too much and too varied material at any one time. Getting organized is a skill most of us work on for years without realizing it; our slow-progressing students will take at least as long, but both they and you will be aware of what is happening and be grateful for small improvements.

Despite the length of this chapter there is much more to know about foundational literacy, particularly specific activities you can use. Fortunately, in the upcoming chapters about expanded literacy you will find activities that are as suitable for slow-progressing students as they are for their more able classmates. With some activities teachers will have to make adaptations, but others invite students to make their own adaptations and, as such, they are the cream of differentiated instruction.

The following vignettes portray real students doing differentiated activities. Better than any activities I could suggest, these vignettes will make clear the characteristics of differentiation for foundational literacy in regular classrooms.

Using Reference Materials

Johnny and Ben are working on one of the two bulletin board quizzes that their teacher, Marlys Sloup, posts every week in her grade 4/5 classroom. Although they have until Friday to finish the quizzes, the boys take pride in being among the first to finish each week. Besides, some questions take a lot of searching or figuring out before they can be answered.

This week there are four groups of questions in the general information quiz. The first group is on the locally designated "Bicycle Month"; it includes questions about scheduled events, safety, theft prevention, and bicycle rental. The second group consists of a pie graph about water distribution on the earth. Children have to pick the most surprising piece of information given by the graph and comment on it. Next, there are three "Winnie the Pooh" comic strips, for which the question is: "Is Eeyore an optimist or a pessimist? Explain why you think so." Finally, there is a group of questions about the West Coast states, California, Oregon, and Washington. It asks about products, earthquakes, the name of the deepest lake, and one state's nickname.

The boys, like many of their classmates, are attracted first to the comic strips. It is easy to understand the point that Eeyore expects the worst to happen, but they do not know if that means he is an *optimist* or a *pessimist*, so they have to consult the classroom dictionary.

The graph problem is fairly easy, too. The surprising fact is that only 5 percent of the earth's water is fresh water. To answer the geography questions, they go to the atlas in the school library but find that they have to consult the encyclopedia and almanac, too.

The Bicycle Month questions send them to back copies of the local newspaper that Mrs. Sloup keeps on a rack. They have to hunt through several issues, but they are familiar enough with the newspaper layout to find the local news quickly. Still, the articles do not answer all the questions. Johnny remembers that there is a poster on bicycle safety hanging in the library, so they go back there to consult it. But how do they find out where to rent bikes? Ben remembers a recent lesson they had on using the Yellow Pages in the phone book. Sure enough! They find the information they need, and the quiz is done.

Nonreaders Do Library Research

Four first graders have come to the library to do research on whales with the help of Karen Austad, the school librarian. Their teacher alerted Ms. Austad yesterday, so she is ready with three books, a file of paintings and photographs, and a large pad of newsprint paper set on an easel.

In a minute they are all seated at a low, round table in the reference corner of the library, out of the flow of traffic of older children looking for fiction.

"What do you already know about whales?" asks Ms. Austad.

"They're big."

"They eat fish."

"There are different kinds."

"They're not really fish."

"Oh? Then what are they?" asks Ms. Austad.

"I don't know."

Ms. Austad writes their information on the newsprint in large manuscript letters under the heading "What we know," Then she asks, "What do you want to find out?"

The answers are slower in coming this time, but gradually the children give voice to their wonderings about whales.

"How much do they weigh?"

"What are they, if they're not fish?"

"How do they breathe?"

"Where do they live?"

"What are the different kinds?"

Ms. Austad writes these questions down, too, this time under the heading, "What we want to find out." Then she says, "I'm going to read some parts from all these books about whales. Listen carefully so we can write a report afterward."

While she reads sections from the books, Ms. Austad shows pictures, stops to explain, and lets the children ask more questions. The books tend to repeat certain facts, but that is all right, since the repetition will help the children to remember. When she is finished reading, Ms. Austad takes a new sheet of newsprint for the "report" the children will now dictate to her.

"What's important to remember?" she asks.

Not surprisingly, the children's interest has shifted from size, weight, and habitat to the fascinating subject of how whales breathe. Taking dictation, Ms. Austad writes down that whales are mammals, that they have lungs, that they breathe out through a blowhole in their heads, that they can stay under water for about an hour but must come to the surface to breathe, that they cannot live long on land because their lungs get crushed. The children would like to have her write more, but she thinks this is enough information for one time. She reads the report aloud, sweeping her hand under the lines. Then the children take turns reading back a line at a time.

Back in their classroom, they will read the report to their classmates and tell any other information that they remember. Then they will copy their report onto smaller paper to put into the class *Animal Reference Book*.

References

CUNNINGHAM, P. M., AND R. L. ALLINGTON. 2003. *Classrooms That Work: They Can All Read and Write.* Boston: Pearson Education.

NESSEL, D., AND J. G. BALTAS. 2000. *Thinking Strategies for Student Achievement.* Arlington Heights, IL: SkyLight Professional Development.

PERSONKE, C., AND D. D. JOHNSON. 1987. *Language Arts and the Beginning Teacher: A Practical Guide.* Englewood Cliffs, NJ: Prentice Hall.

Moving Up and Out With Reading and Writing

Differentiated instruction at its best emerges only when students begin to differentiate their own learning, just as adults differentiate the daily business of their lives. Expecting teachers to design and deliver appropriately leveled and modified activities for all their students all the time is not only asking too much of them, it is also asking too little of students. What we want children and adolescents to do is to take the raw materials of the classroom curriculum and, with guidance from their teachers, mold them into meaningful performances and a continuing quest for knowledge.

In the last chapter I focused on how to help slow-progressing students achieve foundational literacy, without which they cannot exercise the full power of their abilities. In this chapter and the three following, I will examine how students at all levels of literacy can go beyond the fundamentals to work creatively with literature, informational texts, writing, poetry, drama, and projects.

The Teacher's Role

Before we begin, however, I must make clear my philosophical stance on the role of the teacher. In the previous chapter most of the activities suggested were teacher structured because they were intended to help students attain

foundational literacy and meet externally prescribed standards. In such situations, the teacher's job is to make required materials and tasks manageable
for all students either by simplifying them or beefing them up. Sometimes,
she has to take struggling students step by step through a common procedure until they can do it on their own. However, once students are ready to
move beyond the basic requirements, the teacher's job changes. She can
leave much more to student choice and invention. Nevertheless, a teacher
cannot abdicate the responsibility to lead her students, who, because they
are still children, have insufficient experience and knowledge to lead themselves through two thousand years of literature and a wide world of
linguistic culture and communication. In practical terms, this means that a
responsible teacher does not take her class into a library and say, "Pick any
book you want for your projects," but instead provides them with an ample
array of books that are appropriate in content and difficulty for the topics
and forms of their projects. Nor does she leave students to pluck their
writing ideas from the sky. While allowing those who have ideas and plans to
pursue them, she also provides grist for the mills of all class members by
continually bringing new books, current events, human interest stories,
school happenings, and classroom problems to their attention and
suggesting that they write about those things that interest them.

Units for Self-Differentiation

Leading students into self-differentiated reading or writing often means
helping them build a knowledge base in a specific area before taking off on
their own. Reading one story about a new topic or seeing a couple of examples of an unfamiliar type of writing is not enough preparation for young
readers and writers to differentiate their work. That's why I, like many other
educators, prefer extended units to discrete activities. Ideally, units will
relate to and build on each other to form the "umbrella curriculum" previously mentioned. Well-planned units include clusters of fiction and nonfiction books, articles, factual information sources, visual and aural
experiences, and, if possible, artifacts. A unit may start with an attention-
getter, such as a photograph or a song, but it needs to move quickly into an
overview that establishes context, then into interesting bits and pieces that
build familiarity, and finally into serious explorations of included topics.

Generalities are not particularly helpful when talking about units, so
let's focus on a combined literature-social studies unit on pioneer life,
which is often taught in the intermediate grades. Before selecting a long

piece of fiction to read, students need to know where the pioneer territories were, what the terrain and weather were like, and what was involved in communication, obtaining the necessities of life, and travel in the nineteenth century. They should also see pictures or videos of the clothes, tools, furniture, and homes of pioneers. Of course, seeing the real objects in museum displays is even better. When, as an adult, I visited a restored nineteenth-century house in Colorado and saw the furniture and clothing there, I realized for the first time how small people were in pioneer America. When I saw the room where three schoolteachers lived (without heat or running water), prepared their lessons, and slept in one bed, the hardships of life in that place and time finally had meaning for me.

In addition to becoming familiar with a factual background, students need to sample the literature of time and place. The class as a whole ought to read and discuss articles, authentic letters and diary entries, and a book chapter or short story. Only then should you introduce them to the novels available for group study by reading a few pages from each and giving synopses. I would hope that students would have four to six books to choose from, and that there would also be single copies of other novels and nonfiction books for those students who want to read more. As long as I am describing the workings of a specific unit, I will suggest just a few books that can be used in it, too.

Books About Pioneer Life

Sarah, Plain and Tall, by Patricia MacLachlan

Caddie Woodlawn, by Carol Ryrie Brink

Beyond the Divide, by Kathryn Laskey

The Little House series, by Laura Ingalls Wilder

On to Oregon, by Honore Morrow

Wagon Wheels, by Barbara Brenner

A Birthday for Blue, by Kerry Lydon

Save Queen of Sheba, by Louise Moeri

White Captives, by Evelyn Sibley Lampman

The Sign of the Beaver, by Elizabeth George Speare

When students do this type of integrated unit, there is no need for them to be grouped by ability. The activities they will be involved in allow for different levels of understanding and involvement. Students should be able to choose the book they want to read from several introduced by the teacher and, thus, form themselves into heterogeneous groups. Then, each group makes a plan with the teacher for reading their book, discussing it, and designing a culminating activity that will be shared with the class. Although the teacher has a say in what the groups intend to do because she is responsible for their learning and behavior, group members ought to be able to make some choices based on their own inclinations. A group of strong readers may want to read their book straight through individually, and then work together to transform it into a play they can perform for their classmates.

If, on the other hand, a book promises to be tough going for group members, they might want to divide themselves into pairs for reading. Or the group could decide to let each member concentrate on one character as they read and write a diary for that character. Various characters' diary entries organized into a new book would make an absorbing chronicle of the adventures in the original, with an emphasis on point of view. Below is one example of a diary page of a fictional character written by a fourth-grade student.

I have lived my whole life in a movie theater. I eat all the food that people drop on the floor like popcorn and pieces of candy. My favorite food is Wisconsin cheddar cheese. Food is on my mind a lot which is probably why I have the name, Fats. I have two good friends named Raymond the Rat and Marvin the Magnificent.

As you can imagine, I've seen many movies. Gangster movies are our favorite. One day, our leader, Marvin, called us together and said that we were going to go "outside" and "pull a job." I didn't want to go until he said it would be a cheese store and I could have all the Wisconsin cheddar I wanted.

I started the adventure when I cut some holes in a popcorn box that we were going to use as a disguise. We got into the box and when the door to the theater opened, we scooted outside and headed for the cheese shop. And that's when our troubles began.

From: *The Great Cheese Conspiracy* by Jean Van Leeuwen
ALEX BROOKS

Other paths a group might take are:

Group meetings for each chapter, with one member writing up the chapter summary

Selection and preparation of oral readings from the book, with explanatory introductions written by each reader

Research in historical sources to compare the fictional versions of events in their books with factual accounts of the same events, and a panel discussion on the differences

Distillation of important facts from the text in order to prepare a *Jeopardy*-like quiz for classmates

The creation of a comic book version of the story for reluctant readers (which is not as easy as it sounds)

A progressive mural illustrating the action of the book plot

Just how often a group meets and what they do at those meetings are a matter of negotiation among the members and with the teacher. For some books and some groups, twice-weekly meetings with the teacher leading the discussion may be necessary. For others, once a week with the teacher is enough, supplemented by informal meetings where the students lead their own discussion. Having groups working on their own differentiated learning presupposes thorough training in group operation early in the school year. The vignette on the following page illustrates one phase of a self-directed literature study group in action.

Differentiated Contributions to Group Study

As you can see, all these suggested paths have one thing in common: students go through the process of reception, in-processing, storage, out-processing, and production. What you may not have noticed is that the work of each group culminates in a product to be shared with the rest of the class that further enriches their understanding of the overall topic. Another thing that may not be obvious is the extent of self-differentiation going on under the surface of group differentiation. With each student deciding what and how much she should do, some slow-progressing students may not read every page of their book, understand every word, or work on the most demanding parts of the group product, yet they will still be contributing significantly to the group operation. At the same time, those students whose self-differentiation is on a fast track may find that group study opens new paths for them to explore. Armed with a foundation, and given access to other books on the same topic, books by the same authors, and books about pioneering in other times and places, an able student may turn into a history buff.

In this type of self-selected differentiation, when so many different things are going on at so many different levels, teacher leadership is

Fostering Independent Group Skills

Developing children's independent learning is one of Sue Bohlman's main goals in her third-grade reading program. A secondary concern is good use of class time. When she is working with a reading group or conferring with a single child, she wants the other children to be able to carry on productively, not to interrupt or stand waiting for her attention. In her view, giving simple worksheets to keep children busy avoids, rather than solves, the problem. Instead, she has begun to train children to conduct parts of their own reading groups so that she can move among them, taking over when a teacher's guidance is definitely needed or when she wants to demonstrate a procedure the children will soon be expected to handle by themselves.

At this time of year three reading groups are in operation at different stages in their respective trade books. Later on there will be four or even five. The least fluent group, which is reading *Shoe Shine Girl*, by Clyde Bulla, is now reviewing the most recently assigned chapters on its own. The student leader calls on children to read aloud, supplying words when anyone falters. After oral reading she will ask three comprehension questions that Ms. Bohlman has prepared and then write the group's answers or a sheet of paper to be handed in.

The middle group, which has just completed *Key to the Treasure*, by Peggy Parish, is meeting at a round table where the children are writing clues for a treasure hunt to be held on the school playground. They try out their clues on each other to make sure that they are hard enough but not impossible for their classmates.

Children in the most fluent group are finishing their assigned reading in their seats while Ms. Bohlman meets with Christine, their leader. Knowing since last Friday that she would lead all this week, Christine has been reading ahead and planning for discussions. One of her tasks is to pick out three words from each day's reading that might be new for the children in her group. When they meet, she will go over the words in context with the other children, asking them to try to explain what they mean. Now, she explains them to her teacher to demonstrate her own understanding.

Christine's second task is to write a discussion question (called a "think about-talk about question") for each day's group meeting. This is hard for her—indeed for any third grader—since it demands going beyond the literal facts of the story. Ms. Bohlman has been trying to train the children in this high-ability group to recognize that a good discussion question involves interpretation, story relatedness, and uncertainty. It cannot be answered definitely in a few words.

Christine is drawn to an incident in Chapter 7 where Stone Fox hits Willie for no apparent reason. "I'm going to ask what happened in the barn," she says. "There will be plenty to talk about."

"Yes," Ms. Bohlman agrees, "A lot happened in the barn. Will the people in your group have different opinions about what happened?"

"Well, they won't agree on why Stone Fox hit Willie."

"But that isn't your question, is it?"

"And it's related to the rest of the story," argues Christine.

"Tell me how."

"Because Stone Fox felt sorry about it and let Willie win the race."

"How do you know?" asks Ms. Bohlman. "Did Stone Fox or Willie or the author say that?"

"No, I figured it out."

"Well, then, why not ask your question that way, so the others can try figuring it out, too?"

"You mean ask how this part is related to the rest of the story?" Christine thinks for a moment. "It's related to Chapter 6, too, where Stone Fox won't talk to anybody and doesn't trust White people."

"I think your question will get a lot of discussion if you put it that way, Christine."

Christine agrees and starts to write down the question so she will have it ready. In a few minutes Ms. Bohlman calls the group together. She sits down a little distance from them so she can hear without taking any authority away from Christine.

important. While standing in the background, you have to keep an eye on group operation to make sure every student has a role to play and lives up to his responsibilities. You may also have to help a group get organized and stay on track by meeting with the members to talk about problems and ways of solving them. Sometimes, when a group is foundering or speeding toward a dead end, you will have to intervene and straighten things out. Remember, there is a line between giving children time and permission to solve their own problems and abandoning them to endless rounds of trial, error, and discord. The way I see it, if children could teach themselves everything, they wouldn't need teachers or parents and we'd all be out of a job.

Units on Literary Structure and Style

What about the teacher's goals in all this self-differentiation, you may wonder. Groups designing their own study plans and projects may not pay much attention to aspects of literacy that their teachers think are important, such as the traditionally taught elements of literature: plot structure, setting, character development, mood, and theme. Well, the short answer is that not everything about literacy can be taught in one unit. Recognizing that students will not always choose to pursue what she has in mind, the teacher needs to remember that there are other units in an umbrella curriculum. The unit on pioneer life, described earlier, is based on social studies, which—like science—tends to be studied topically. Literature, on the other hand, can be studied thematically, structurally, stylistically, or qualitatively. To have students do any of these types of study, you need to develop units specifically for that purpose. You will have to cluster materials differently, provide a different kind of background information, and probably increase the amount of sampling students do because, for the first time, they are studying the workings of literature, not looking through literature to study something else. Although students may still form their own groups, choose their own books, and decide on their own products, their paths of study will need more teacher guidance and supervision. I expect that at least some meetings of all groups will be teacher-led.

An example of a literary analysis unit is in order. I won't pick character study because so many teachers are already familiar with that type of unit, but instead will describe a unit on form and style. As adults, we know that different authors choose to handle similar material in different ways, although we don't think much about how or why they do it. Children, who have much less experience with literature than we do, tend to take each piece they read as a natural event, without any awareness that choices were made by an unseen author. Through the study of different representations of the same and similar stories, students can begin to comprehend the kinds of decisions that go into writing and what it means to be a writer. A rich source for teaching form and style to students of any age is traditional literature that was once part of an oral culture and was later written down: fairy tales, folktales, myths, legends, and fables. Any of these genres can be studied by primary-grade students, the similarities and differences in versions of stories jumping off the page and shouting, "Look at me." They can also be taught in high school. As described, here, however, the unit is intended for middle schoolers.

If the teacher decides to focus on fairy tales, he will find that not only are there several different versions of popular fairy tales in any library, but there are also books in which authors have brought together different tellings of tales from a particular country and related stories from other parts of the world. These resources will be more than adequate for teaching a fairy tale unit.

Middle schoolers will not be instantly enthralled by this choice of content, which they normally connect with very young children. The teacher has to make clear at the outset that what they are doing is studying literary form and style through a ready and easily understandable source. The object is to have them learn about some qualities of good writing, and the anticipated products are stories of their own creation. To emphasize the purpose of the unit the teacher starts by reading aloud a new and an old version (in that order) of a familiar tale, such as "Little Red Riding Hood." (If this story in its original form seems too gory and sexually suggestive for middle school students, he can exchange it for something milder, such as "Beauty and the Beast" or "Cinderella.") Afterward, he asks students to point out the differences between the two versions and talk about the effects on the story as a whole. For example, in some newer versions of "Little Red Riding Hood," Grandmother pops out of the wolf's body unharmed after the woodsman has killed it; in older ones, she stays dead. Sometimes her remains are even described as part of the wolf's stomach contents. The first treatment is certainly more upbeat and easier on the psyches of children.

At this point the teacher should give the class some of the historical background of fairy tales to help them understand their origins and how changes in them occurred. The violence and harshness of many of the originals can be explained by the fact that they were not intended to entertain, but to teach moral and practical lessons in dangerous times.

Students need to do a lot of sampling before they are ready to create tales of their own. Typically, children get to know only a few of the most popular fairy tales, and then only in their general outlines. In this unit middle schoolers should read tales they have never heard of before, as told by the Brothers Grimm or the French compiler of tales, Charles Perrault. They should also read the more recent and original tales of Hans Christian Andersen, sample modern writers' interpretations and spoofs of familiar tales, and get at least a taste of tales from the Middle East and the Orient. Because so many different routes through this large body of literature are possible, the teacher will probably want to create groups at this point. Again, the groups can be formed by student choice, and groups can share their learning through a culminating activity. The goal is for students to experience the comparisons and contrasts between tales that reveal form and style.

When it comes to writing fairy tales, students have several possibilities for self-differentiation. They may choose to write their own version of an existing tale, devise a new ending for an old tale, turn a serious tale into a comedy or satire, or create an entirely original story. They also have the option of working alone or with a collaborator. (Group story writing usually doesn't work out. In this case, too many cooks really do spoil the broth.) As with all units where students create something, products should be shared. Below is a piece written by a fourth-grade girl after reading a version of "Little Red Riding Hood."

Today is another terrible day. It's a beautiful day with the sun shining but I can't get out of bed with this cold. I can't get any rest because the woodsman is chopping down trees and is making so much noise. No one is coming to visit me today way out here in the forest and I'm too weak to cook my own meals. I think it's time to move into the city. As soon as I'm better I'll leave these noisy and dangerous woods.

Yesterday I was lying in bed when I heard someone knocking at the door. I asked who it was and the voice said, "Little Red." I told her to come right in but instead of dear Little Red, it was the wolf!

Fortunately I managed a scream before the wolf had totally gobbled me up. The woodsman heard my scream, came and killed the wolf and got me out. Being eaten by a wolf is a most dreadful thing! It was the last straw! I have had it with these woods!

I will ask my daughter to help me move to town where I can have my own little house and garden and people nearby. Maybe I can sell the extra things I grow at the market. Best of all, there will certainly be no wolves!

Jessica Spiegel

Beyond writing their own tales, a few students may be drawn to research on fairy tales or other traditional forms of literature. One fascinating exploration is the use of structural patterns in traditional literature, such as the use of "threes": three tasks, three questions, three suitors, three siblings, and so on. Why do they appear over and over again, and show up in stories from different parts of the world? Are there times when these patterns represent something cultural or psychological rather than being just a rhetorical convenience? In attempting to answer such questions, novice researchers can make good use of the same books the teacher used to develop the unit.

As I mentioned, this type of unit can be scaled up or down for students of different ages. High school students, who've had more exposure to a variety of traditional forms of literature, should be able to trace the development of a particular form without a teacher leading the way and produce sophisticated pieces of writing. A good place for a high school class to begin a unit is with "Sir Gawain and the Green Knight," a fourteenth-century literary masterpiece that embodies many of the characteristics and devices of the oral tradition. In the primary grades, teachers can use simple modern renditions of fairy tales to teach reading, and then examine two or three versions with their students, helping them to find the differences and understand their effects. Later, if given a familiar plot structure, young children will be able to use it to write their own fairy tales. In most cases, we can expect them to produce something like "Curlytop and the Three Bunnies" rather than an original tale. As an illustration of what young children are capable of, I offer an unedited story written long ago by a first grader (my son) after he had read a bunch of fairy tales in school. I suspect he was also influenced by television adventure shows, however.

The Bat Who Eats Chilbren
RICHIE YATVIN

One day some chilbren went for a walk in the woods. It was dark in the woods. In the woods there was a cave with a bat in it. The bat loved to eat chilbren. Then the children came nearer the cave. The bat saw the children come. The bat jumped out of his cave. The bat said, "Who are you?"

"Oh we are children who came into the woods to take a walk."

"Oh I see," said the bat. "I'm the bat who loves to eat children."

The children said, "Then we have to go!"

"Yes," said the bat. "You go away from my cave or I will eat you kids."

"Nobody will make us go away, you bat!"

"So do you want to be eaten up by me?"

"Go ahead," said the children.
"O.K. you said it." "Here I go."
"Go ahead."
"All right, you asked for it!"
So the bat started to eat the children up.

Writing as a Separate Activity

Both the units I've described involve students in reading, writing, speaking, and listening—not to mention research and projects. But I would like to devote some special attention to writing, apart from any unit. Since all acts of writing are self-differentiated, I could confine my comments to an endorsement of writers' workshop and be done with the subject. If I did only that, however, I feel would be shortchanging my readers, their students, and the art of writing that I care so much about. I believe that teaching writing includes guided writing experiences as well as free writing. Regularly, teachers need to present models of good writing, examine them with students, and ask students to incorporate key elements into their own writing. Students, as self-differentiators, will use models in different ways and to different extents. Some will take a writer's basic plot or argument as is, and just substitute different characters or events. Others will pick out the things they like best, such a first-person narrator or flashbacks, and leave the rest. In between will lie a range of borrowing and original thinking.

My beliefs about teaching writing from models are based on two principles: language is a socially constructed process; and written and spoken language are different. What the first principle means is that a language is invented—and changed—by the members of a community. (I use the term *community* here to refer to groups of language users as small as a family and as large as a country. As people mature, they are likely to join several overlapping language communities, but we each have a "home" community that exerts the greatest influence over us while we are young.) Children growing up in a particular community learn the forms of its language—everything from phonemes to rituals and metaphors—by interacting with more mature community members. Children do not learn language in isolation the way they learn to walk and to use their hands as tools. The second principle means that the oral and written strands of a language employ different structures, devices, and conventions to express the thoughts behind them. For example, written language uses sentences (most of the time), while oral language may just as often, and just as legitimately, use fragments and run-ons.

The problems children have with writing in school stem from one or more of the following sources:

1. Immaturity, that is, not yet having sufficient knowledge of the forms and vocabulary of one's own language community

2. Confusing the oral and written forms of language, thus using speech conventions when they should be using writing conventions

3. Belonging to a home community whose language practices are at odds with those of the larger community

We see these various sources of difficulty reflected in such descriptions as "Your drawing is cool, ya know, like awesome"; in the excessive use of "and" as an all-purpose connector; and in the grammatically improper use of "them" and "us" as the subjects of sentences. Yes, I know that with time and experience most students move beyond these faltering attempts at written expression. But, pardon me if I don't believe that writing practice, even when it is combined with reflection and feedback, is the mechanism that enables them to do it. I am much more inclined to credit their unconscious assimilation of the characteristics of high-quality literature and their conscious attempts to imitate them. Like Frank Smith, I believe that "we learn to write by reading."

My recommendations, then, for differentiated instruction in writing are to immerse students in written language, examine all kinds of published writing with students from a writer's point of view, and use the best of those pieces as models for writing. Literature, I believe, should be the mainstay of any writing program, but students should also become familiar with journalistic pieces, advertisements, book and movie reviews, greeting cards, travel brochures and other components of popular culture. Each type of writing, with its own form and style, is worthy of student examination and imitation. Here are some examples of children's writing modeled on nonliterary forms:

Eleven-Year-Old Discovered in Army

A shocking discovery was made Wednesday at the Green Beret basic training camp in Oklahoma City. One of the lieutenants found out that recruit Jason Manderino was only eleven years old. Reporters have had difficulty getting on the base because the army is trying to keep the matter quiet.

Alice Martin from Madison, Wisconsin had found out the story from her boyfriend in the same unit that an eleven year old was in the army. Young Jason was discovered when a lieutenant had found his birth certificate and noticed that the year had been changed from 1972 to 1962.

It is surprising that Manderino passed the tests. He is tall and looks old for his age. He is also smart and muscular. The army must be embarrassed about the situation. I wonder where Jason will show up next.

A Treat Spreader

Have you ever had a time in your life when you ate the last candy bar or a last piece of popcorn and you wished there were more? Well, have I got news for you. My new machine will let you eat your same treats over and over again.

First take the treat spreader box, stick in your last piece of treat, count to five, push the button on the top, wait ten seconds, open the box and there will be double of what you put in.

Order now. You may get the special low price of $27.30. Guaranteed. This special offer will last only two weeks. The machine cannot be broken.

Mrs. Green from Alaska was having a party for fifty. She had one piece of popcorn. She doubled it to a thousand, in just twenty minutes.

For primary-grade children, literature is the main source of ideas and models of form and style. There is a wealth of simple books that, while not literary masterpieces, are of sufficient quality to be used as models for writing. One that works very well is Judith Viorst's *Alexander and the Terrible, Horrible, No Good, Very Bad Day.* Because Alexander's experiences and feelings are so much like those of real children (and adolescents), novice writers eagerly adopt Viorst's plot format to describe their own days. Here is one example written by a seven-year-old girl.

Mercedes and the Super, Terrific, Phenomenal, Very Good Day

My mom took me ice skating and then she took me to a restaurant for lunch. I knew it was going to be a super, terrific, phenomenal, very good day. Then she took me to one of my friend's houses. After that she took me home to get ready for my bird's birthday. I wore my pink dress. I knew it was going to be a super, terrific, phenomenal, very good day. I got to watch my favorite T.V. show. When I went to bed, I got right to sleep. It was a super, terrific, phenomenal, very good day.

Simple children's books can be used with older students, too. In my experience, upper elementary students do not balk at this kind of activity; they think it is fun, especially when they get to do illustrations, too. Below is a list of some other primary-level books that can be used as models for writing throughout the elementary grades.

It Looks Like Spilled Milk

Q is for Duck,

What Do You Say, Dear

Fortunately, Unfortunately

If You Give a Mouse a Cookie

The Very Hungry Caterpillar

Mary Wore Her Red Dress

Jesse Bear, What Will You Wear?

Oh, Lovely Mud

Longer, more advanced books do not make good models because there are too many aspects of form and style for young writers to consider all at once, but you can take a short section or even a chapter. Think about the episode with the Cheshire cat or the one with Tweedle Dum and Tweedle Dee in the Alice in Wonderland books. Think about the first page of *Tuck Everlasting,* in which the seasons of the year are described. For older students other short forms of literature, such as essays, letters, and short stories, are also suitable.

I am going to end this chapter with three more examples of children's writing that show what students can do when encouraged to use models as the basis for self-differentiating their writing. What makes these different from the previous examples is that these intermediate-grade writers have moved far away from the original models into the realm of creativity. In these cases, I don't even know what the originals were.

Teayas the Stallion

Many moons ago there was a herd of horses. Teayas the stallion, who was the leader of the herd, was taking the herd south to find more food. But Teayas did not know that the herd was heading straight toward a huge fire. By the time Teayas sensed the fire, the fire had spread all around them. But Teayas did not waste time. He immediately gathered his herd. The only way out was through the fire, so Teayas and the herd ran right through the flames. And ever since that time, horses have always had flames on the back of their necks and on their tails.

Complaints of My Desk

Dear Glenn,

You always drop my top jaw and you never clean my mouth! Sometimes someone writes on me. I get moved out of position and I'm stuffed! You always kick my feet and you put your elbows on my face. I'm getting tired of you slamming your chair into me, and besides, how do you think it feels? It hurts, right chair? Yeah. How would you feel if a pencil dropped on your head every ten seconds? I hate it! Why do you stick your hand into my mouth? Next time you do that I'll bite your hand.

Your desk

The Prayer of the Wolf

Dear Good Spirits,

Thank you for rabbits, mice, and caribou that make us strong. I'm especially grateful for the courage you give me to lead the wolf pack. When my pack needs me, I'm there. We don't kill any more animals than we need to. I'm going to ask for a couple of things. I just have one question first. Why did you make people so afraid of us? People shoot and kill us for no good reason. Good Spirits, please don't let people kill anyone in my family. Please keep my family safe from men and other dangers. Amen

References

NORTON, D. E. 1991. *Through the Eyes of a Child: An Introduction to Children's Literature.* New York: McMillan.

———. *Pencil Power, 1984: Collected Poems, Stories, and Sketches from the Primary Grades.* Madison, WI: Crestwood Elementary School.

Routman, R. 1999. *Conversations: Strategies for Teaching, Learning, and Evaluation.* Portsmouth, NH: Heinemann.

SMITH, F. 1994. *Understanding Reading: A Psycholinguistic Analysis of Reading and Learning to Read, Fifth Edition.* Hillsdale, NJ: Lawrence Erlbaum Associates.

———. *Soaring and Exploring with the Author in Me: Compositions by Students in Grades 4-5, 1983-1984.* Madison, WI: Crestwood Elementary School.

———. *Soaring and Exploring with the Author in Me: Compositions by Students in Grades 4-5, 1988.* Madison, WI: Crestwood Elementary School.

6

Drama as a Way to Learn

The minor place of drama in the elementary and middle school literacy curriculum has always puzzled me. Not only is drama a powerful tool for students to increase their oral language competence, it is also a good way for them to practice the reception-production process, using both oral and written language. In addition, drama is so appealing to students of all ages that teachers do not have to "motivate" them to get involved. Self-differentiation forms the icing on this delicious cake, since students need very little help from their teachers in creating a variety of dramatic experiences for themselves.

The allure of drama for children is that it is an ever ready opportunity to act out all the experiences they like best, dread most, or would like to have. Drama is the transformation of all their daydreams into an almost-reality that increases pleasure and reduces pain. For teachers, the appeal of drama is in its adaptability for teaching. Ordinary literacy activities don't provide enough opportunities for students to use oral language or to transform written language into oral language. Classroom drama does that and more, helping students to increase their vocabularies, improve their grammar and usage, and learn the appropriate language forms for different social occasions. It also introduces students to new and interesting ways to receive, process, store, and produce written language. Thus, drama is the vehicle for accomplishing a number of instructional goals in ways that students will not think of as work.

For all these reasons teachers should embrace classroom drama. In this chapter, I will discuss many of the ways you can involve students in dramatic activities without getting tangled in the artistic demands of teaching acting or the technical demands of producing a theatrical performance. As in the previous chapter, the emphasis will be on self-differentiation: students using drama to help themselves understand literature, culture, history, and human behavior and to express their understandings creatively in a new form.

Dramatic Improvisation

The easiest type of classroom drama is dramatic improvisation: choosing a situation, then acting it out with language and movement. Young children do this on their own all the time, playing house, playing school, pretending to be ghosts or other supernatural creatures, or simulating the adventures of action heroes. To some extent, children's dramatic improvisations have stories, but the stories tend to ramble on and diverge as each child follows his own impulses. Living inside a situation as someone else seems to be more important to young children than getting somewhere with a story. In the classroom, dramatic improvisation is more structured than in spontaneous play, since the teacher's aim is to have children act in concert, responding to one another and using mature language.

In the beginning, at least, the teacher chooses the situation and sets it moving through questions and suggestions. If children seem too uncertain to plunge into dramatic action, the teacher may decide to support them by taking a role herself. For example, in working with a small group of first graders, a teacher might use the familiar classroom playhouse with its table, dishes, and such to develop a before-school scenario. She could say, "It's eight o'clock. The school bus will be here soon, Mom and Dad have to leave for work, and nobody has had breakfast yet. Jane, you be the mom; Chris, you're the dad; I'll be one of the kids, and Rich, you be my brother. The rest of you are the audience this time. What should we do? What do we say to each other?"

Before beginning to dramatize this situation, the whole group needs to talk and plan. Will the family eventually get to eat their breakfast? Will the children make the bus? Who is going to do what? As a member of the group, the teacher participates fully in this discussion. Although the group needs to reach consensus about how the story will play out, the details of the action and the words spoken are up to the actors.

A situation should be enacted two or three times with different children playing the parts, so that the group can make changes and additions. You will want to make sure that any child who has only a small part in the first enactment gets to play a major role later on; and you withdraw as the children gain confidence. With each enactment, the scene will probably get longer and the action and dialogue more elaborate. That means that the actors are thinking through their roles and trying to make them more real. After each dramatization, the group discusses the actors' interpretation, the differences from other dramatizations, and the special qualities that stood out. Praise of any sort is welcome, but only three types of criticism should be permitted: "I couldn't hear you"; "I couldn't see what you were doing"; and "I didn't understand what was happening." Dramatic improvisation before an audience is a form of communication. The actors have to do their best to communicate, and the audience has to let them know when they are and are not successful. If there are a lot of problems, a group can work on them and perform their piece again.

As children become familiar with the format of dramatic improvisation, they can begin to differentiate their own scenes without the teacher's involvement. At this stage, three to five actors may work together to plan and rehearse their own version of a given situation. The whole group meets for the performances and the follow-up discussion. Ultimately, children should be able to find their own situations in literature, classroom happenings, or their lives outside of school and dramatize them with little teacher assistance. Some groups of children may want to set aside a weekly time for improvised drama; others will prefer to use drama as interesting situations arise.

Working with Older Students

With older students, teachers will be more successful if they select situations with significant and clearly defined problems. Although problem dramatizations can range from the realistic to the wildly improbable, intermediate grade and middle school students feel more comfortable starting out with ones they have actually faced, such as how to deal with a bully on the playground or how to persuade their parents to let them do something heretofore forbidden. The process is the same as it is for young children: group discussion, consensus, two or three enactments with different actors, and debriefing. Older students are less likely to need the teacher involved as an actor, and they will be able to move more quickly than younger ones to the stages of working out and developing their own scenarios.

I must argue for using teacher-suggested situations, at least part of the time. Since the purposes of dramatic improvisation in classrooms are the development of oral language and understanding of human behavior, students need to be guided toward situations that will take them into unfamiliar territory. One type of scenario that is very important, and that students might not choose on their own, is the "higher rung on the social ladder" situation. In such a scenario, students assume the roles of people who are more grown up, wealthy, sophisticated, or educated than they are. The situation could be a cocktail party, a job interview, an encounter with a famous person, a disciplinary conference with the school principal, or anything where one or more characters would be expected to speak like cultured adults. Working under the implicit demand for refined language and formal behavior, students will do their best to rise to the occasion, employing vocabulary and grammatical structures that they've heard or read but do not normally use. Even though the results may be awkward or incorrect, the experience is valuable for all students and should be repeated frequently.

On the more imaginative side, students of all ages can benefit from working through situations where the characters are from different times, places or universes. How would fictional characters such as Count Dracula, Wonder Woman, or Robin Hood talk? What about angels or elves or fairy godmothers? What will students talk like thirty years from now? There are countless possibilities for self-differentiation in imaginative situations and social class situations that should should not be missed just because students don't think of them first.

Dramatizing Literature

Another type of structured classroom drama is the transformation of pieces of literature into dramatic scenes or full plays. I am not talking about Readers Theater, which relies heavily, if not completely, on speaking the exact written text. In transformational drama activities students assimilate a written text and then reconstruct it in dramatic form using their own language. This type of drama requires and demonstrates students' reception, processing, storage, and production of language and can, in fact, be used as an informal assessment of these skills.

While reading a story to a primary class, a teacher may stop after an exciting part and ask if any children want to act out what she has just read. More commonly, however, the teacher will work with a small group of children, allowing them to finish reading and talking about a story before suggesting that they act it out. This kind of dramatization doesn't need planning like a dramatic improvisation because everyone knows in advance how the story goes. A story may be dramatized once or several times, depending on the group's enthusiasm for it. They may like their own creation so well that they want to polish it and perform it for the whole class. In that case, there must be a role for each person or two versions presented, so that no group member is relegated to the job of stagehand. The actors will need to rehearse a few times to get everything coordinated, but they do not memorize their speeches. As with dramatic improvisation, you want students to make changes in what they say as they get more familiar with the material and come to a better understanding of the characters they are playing. You also want them to be attentive to what the other actors say and do, and respond appropriately.

I can remember an incident from my early years of teaching when my first graders were presenting their version of "Hansel and Gretel" to a whole school audience. Performing in the round, with minimal costumes and few props, the actors were unself-consciously living the story as they acted. When the child playing the witch got stuck going into the cardboard box representing the oven, "Gretel" didn't hesitate. She gave her a good shove and said in a very irritated voice, "Stop stalling, you old witch!" That bit brought down the house.

After some experience with improvised dialogue, students may want to write out their plays. Writing of this kind can be done by a group if each member takes a character and dictates his or her lines to a scribe who writes them all down and adds stage directions. When you are aiming for quality, however, it is better to have students write in pairs than in groups or alone. In group writing, coherence is often lost because each writer/character is concentrating on his own lines. And in solitary writing, there is no child acting as critic to bring a wandering writer back on track. Another possible difficulty with group writing is that the more capable students will write themselves the biggest and juiciest parts and leave little for their classmates to do. Hearkening back to the advice on grouping in Chapter 2, teachers need to monitor group process regularly and make sure that every member has an opportunity to contribute and shine. Even though all parts may not be equal in length, they should all be interesting and allow each character some moments at center stage.

In the next vignette is an example of a very simple play, transformed from a story and written down by two second-grade boys. Notice how criticism from one partner helps the process work as it should.

Creating a Puppet Play

A group of second graders has been reading the Frog and Toad books by Arnold Lobel. Because the plots are simple, and there is a lot of dialogue, these books are good for various kinds of dramatizations. Today, the teacher, Nancy Curtin, has paired off the children to write their own plays about Frog and Toad. They may use a situation from one of the books or make up an original one based on the kinds of activities Frog and Toad usually do and the ways they behave. The children will plan a plot, write down the lines, make stick puppets, and rehearse. Next Tuesday they will visit all the other primary classrooms to present their plays for the children.

David and Ross, who are working together, have decided to make their puppets first. While they draw and color them, they talk about their play.

DAVID: *Let's do the story where Frog and Toad go swimming.*
RUSS: *Nah. That's too long. And it has all those other animals in it. We'd have to make maybe ten puppets.*
DAVID: *We can change it and make it short. They can build a diving board.*
RUSS: *Okay. You be Frog, and I'll be Toad because I want to be silly.*
DAVID: *How are you going to be silly?*
RUSS: *I don't know yet. Let's just make the puppets talk.*
DAVID AS FROG: *Let's go swimming.*
ROSS AS TOAD: *It's too cold. Let's wait for a warm day.*
DAVID: *This isn't going to work, if you won't let them go swimming.*
Ross: *Okay, okay. Start again.*

Here is the final version of the play written by David and Ross.

The Diving Board
— WRITTEN BY DAVID PRIEST & ROSS CURKEET

F: *Oh, such a lovely spring day.*
T: *Yes! Let's go swimming.*
F: *O.K. Toad. Where will we go?*
T: *To the pond, of course. (Down they go to the pond.)*
T: *Let's make a diving board, O.K.?*
F: *O.K. I will get a saw. (Frog went away and came back with a saw.)*
T: *Let's cut down that big tree. (The two friends cut down the biggest tree and make it into a smooth board.)*
F: *I will get a hammer and some nails.*
T: *O.K. I will wait here. (Frog brought a hammer and nails back.)*
F: *How come you are eating flies?*
T: *I just got hungry and had a little snack.*
F: *Let's get to work.*
T: *O.K. (The two friends nail the board on a stump.) We're finally done!*
F: *Yes! Let's go swimming now.*
T: *O.K. (They go swimming all day long.)*

Stumbling Blocks in Playwriting

This example suggests one of the stumbling blocks that students often meet in transforming stories into plays. The boys had to change the events in the original story because they were too difficult to dramatize. Many stories present similar problems in the forms of time, distance, and action that can't be realistically shown. Teachers have to be on the lookout for such obstacles and help their students figure out ways to overcome them. One device that is often used in plays is a narrator or a chorus who tells what can't be dramatized. Another device is symbolic representation, such as a sign reading, "At the beach" or a cardboard moon that is carried across the stage to represent the passing of a night. I have also seen travel represented by scenery that moved while characters walked in place. Inventing such devices for their plays is good practice in differentiated learning for students. But teachers also have to help students recognize that some stories are just not suitable for dramatization.

With older students the main stumbling block is the urge to take on too much. You can't collapse a two-hundred-page novel into a twenty-minute play, but that's exactly what many intermediate grade students want to do. Transforming single incidents into dramatic scenes as they read through a book doesn't have the same appeal for them as it does for primary-grade children. The best compromise I can suggest for an intermediate grade or middle school group planning a culminating activity for a novel they've enjoyed, is to pick one or two scenes for dramatization and appoint a narrator to give an overview of the rest of the book.

There is an additional difficulty inherent in mature literature that also trips up older would-be playwrights. That is the use of literary stylistic elements, such as flashbacks, internal monologues, and detailed descriptions. When transforming stories that have those elements, writers have to interpret incidents rather than try to represent them literally. In so doing, they may need to omit some things from the dialogue and rely on the skills of actors to communicate them with movement and facial expression. Clearly, older students are then edging into the realm of drama as art. If that is where they want to go, I would not discourage them. Nor would I deny them the opportunity to present their creations to an audience. The plays that emerge from such an intense interest in drama are the hoped-for products of self-differentiated learning. But at the same time, these plays often require elaborate scenery, costumes, props, lighting, sound effects, and polished acting. Bringing all those things together is a major project for students and their teachers. It may be worth doing once or twice a year, but regularly devoting large amounts of class time to preparing full-scale productions involving only a few members of the class is not a practical pedagogical decision. If the situation arises, a teachers can arrange for the thespians to rehearse after school or during the noon hour and offer them occasional advice, but this is a project students have to pursue on their own.

Let's turn away from dramatizing literature now and look at more mundane applications that also offer opportunities for differentiated learning. Students can learn a great deal about the subject matter of various disciplines by synthesizing factual information into a dramatic presentation or watching a presentation by their classmates. Although I am not a fan of dramatized lessons in which children become foods to teach nutrition or numbers to teach math, I enjoy seeing history, geography, and civics come alive in dramas that children have conceived.

Two kinds of drama are possible in these areas, each with numerous variations: (1) realistic enactments of actual events with real people as the characters, such as the signing of the Declaration of Independence; and (2) imaginative enactments of hypothetical situations rooted in factual information, such as a slice of daily life in a Northwest Native American community in the nineteenth century. As you can see, the first kind of drama applies mostly to history, although the historical aspects of art or science could also be dramatized. The second kind works for history and geography, but is most useful for civics. Through dramatic enactments, students can come to understand how trials, elections, town meetings, and other societal institutions work far better than by just reading about them.

Both types of drama require students to do careful research. They have to do a lot of reading and gathering of data to create an accurate enactment. Building background knowledge and seeing models are also important. What students are trying to represent is too far removed from their own lives for them to be able to imagine the details without visual, aural, and tactile points of reference. So the teacher needs to provide photos, paintings, and artifacts for context, and movies or plays to show how adult professionals created enactments. Hundreds of historical and geographical films are available at public libraries and museums. There are some excellent commercial films, too. I suggest that teachers rent *Quest for Fire* (1981) from their local video store and study it as an example of an imaginative enactment based on archaeological and anthropological data. Be warned, however, that this film is not for your students. It has some sex and violence in it that are not appropriate for school showing. I mention it here only because it is the best example of its type that I have ever seen, and I think you should see it, too.

Realistic and imaginative enactments do not need scripts. When students construct them—in groups, this time—they outline the events to be depicted and catalogue the details under each event. For example, if they are going to enact a Chinook (a Northwest tribe) potlatch, they will list each part of the festival in sequence, and under each part note who will speak or perform an action and what props will be needed. All the details should be discussed and checked against the references used. But the characters' speeches are best improvised to insure naturalness and human interest.

The study of history and geography suggests another type of dramatization which is not quite drama. It is simulation of an entire sequence of events through role playing. It involves some acting and use of clothing and props, but its mainstay is written dramatization: letters, diaries, and autobiographical essays. These are essentially dramatic because in them students focus on action and characters and take on a role that is different from their real selves. The vignette on the next page describes part of a simulation unit that involves writing in imaginative roles.

Obviously, with its dependence on facts and details, this kind of drama is most appropriate for intermediate and middle school students. At a very simple level, however, it can be used in the primary grades. Think mostly about enacting community situations, such as doing business at the bank or post office, or voting. Young children also do well with fictionalized history, such as the celebration of the first Thanksgiving and Betsy Ross sewing the first American flag. In addition, they can enact family scenes about life in other countries they have read about (see page 91).

Dramatizing with Puppets

Any of the types of classroom drama described above can be performed with puppets rather than live actors. Puppets have some advantages we might not recognize immediately, especially for dramatizing fantasy literature. They can do many things in dramatizations that are impossible for child actors: climb beanstalks, slay dragons and villains, lift enormous weights, and fly. More important, however, puppets can be the uninhibited surrogates for self-conscious children. Sometimes, there are a few students in a class who avoid dramatization altogether because they are too shy to perform before an audience. At other times students will start to create a play around a story and then run into a character that no one wants to portray. More often, dramatized situations include ideas and attitudes, such sex or race discrimination, that students do not want to be identified with. In all these instances, students would be willing to be the voices and movers behind puppets who assume the unpopular roles.

Role Playing Along the Oregon Trail

For several weeks all the grade 4 and 5 classes will be engaged in a simulation of pioneers traveling west by wagon train in the 1840s. As part of the simulation, the children have chosen identities, organized themselves into families, and elected leaders. Given the limitations of weight and space within their wagons, they have had to choose which treasured personal possessions they will take and decide what new supplies and equipment are necessary. As background they have read books about the dangers from Indians, wagon breakdowns, disease, and lack of water. Finally, there has been a lot of discussion about the route they will take, their plan of travel, and how they will meet problems along the way.

Now, as they start their imaginary journey, they are also starting diaries of their experiences. In the diaries, each child plays the role of the person she or he has chosen, with a name, a background, a family, a profession, a personality, and hopes for a new life in Oregon. As they meet the hardships and arrive at the places determined by the pattern of the simulation, they record events and feelings in their diaries, trying to see them through the eyes of the people who lived the trip. Below are diary entries written by two children, reflecting both the reality of the trip and the personalities they have assumed.

I'm going to Oregon. I decided in a very odd way. In fact, I reckon I hadn't thought much about the trip until about 2 weeks ago. I was working in my store when customers started pouring in. I asked a customer what the mob was about and he told me everybody's going to Oregon.

I yelled, "Thunderation! What a great idea. They'll need good stores in Oregon!" So I decided to go. I hope to meet some Cherokees and friendly Indians but I don't want no trouble from them Chickamaugas.

I have high hopes to reach Oregon before winter. I plan to leave from Independence, Missouri around April 30th. I pray that I have a good and safe trip.

—*JEFF SCHWARTZ*

Barroom! The big drum was being hit to wake up all the people in our camp.

Big Bubba Sutter (our wagon master) was starting to line up the wagons so we could get out of Independence first.

I think we all needed a little more sleep because Bubba started to turn the wagons east. Jennifer Smith was trying to get her children ready and one year old Tom found interest in a cow's hind leg and got kicked. When we took the poor fella to the doctor he had a broken arm and bruises all over. We had troubles like being at the end of the line and trying to pass people and getting stuck in gullies or holes. When we finally arrived here at about ten it was hard to find a place to stop for the night. Tomorrow I will be writing again. Goodbye.

—*JENNY BRIGHTBILL*

Being Drama Ready

In this chapter, I have not tried to exhaust all the possibilities for drama in the classroom. You may have noticed that I've said nothing about plays written by adults for children. That's because commercially written, scripted plays do not leave much room for differentiated learning. The best you can say of them is that they have parts of varying length and difficulty. Once teachers get started with drama they will find many other dramatic experiences that have more potential than prepared scripts. The content of math, science, and other subjects can often be made clearer and more memorable through dramatization. Sometimes students need to do real-life role playing in order to understand how others feel or how they should act in difficult situations. There are also poems and songs that just beg to be acted out. You should be ready to take advantage of all these "teachable moments." And you will be if you make drama a regular part of the curriculum, have puppets and simple props on hand, and remember that you are not teaching acting or drama as art. All types of improvised and student-authored drama can enrich the classroom experience, increasing students' literacy competence and their ability to differentiate their own learning.

References

BARNES, D. 1976. *From Communication to Curriculum.* Harmondsworth, UK: Penguin.

CHAMBERS, D. 1970. *Storytelling and Creative Drama.* Dubuque, IA: William C. Brown.

STEWIG, J. W., AND CAROL BUEGE. 1994. *Dramatizing Literature in Whole Language Classrooms.* New York: Teachers College Press.

WARD, W. 1957. *Playmaking with Children.* New York: Appleton-Century-Crofts.

Waxing Poetic

Gone are the days when all students were required to memorize a couple of classic or patriotic poems each year without ever quite understanding them. Today, children may learn a well-loved poem by heart, but their work with poetry encompasses so much more that is personal and creative that memorization is merely a footnote. First, students enjoy reading scores of poems during their school careers, many of them related to the curriculum, but also many others that they choose themselves. Second, most of the poems they encounter have been written for children or young people, reflecting their feelings and experiences and using their language. The most important difference, however, is that children create their own poetry as a regular classroom activity instead of just appreciating the work of published poets.

In devoting this chapter to differentiating with poetry, I feel I have only a little to add to what differentiating teachers already know and do. And yet, I hope you will find these small additions valuable in expanding the range of poetry students experience, in increasing their understanding of poetry, and in raising the quality of the poetry they produce.

Understanding Poetry

Differentiated instruction in poetry offers three possibilities. Students can

1.   read and collect the poems that appeal to their tastes and interests.

2. read aloud or recite their favorite poems to others.

3. compose their own poems.

The teacher's job is to introduce students to a rich and varied array of poems that will help them understand the nature and characteristics of good poetry. In my work in classrooms, I have observed that students of all ages tend to misunderstand what poetry is because they have not read enough poems or enough variety of poems. When asked, they will tell you that poetry is a story that rhymes, a bunch of beautiful words, or advice about how to live our lives. Sometimes they will name the haiku or the cinquain as a kind of poetry they know about, but they think of those forms only as arbitrary controls on the number of syllables one can use. Thus, when they try to write their own poems, the pieces often turn out to be doggerel, moral platitudes, or romanticized depictions of nature.

Real poems often tell stories, evoke strong visual images, or present noble truths, but none of those qualities is the essence of poetry. Poetry is an organic design made up of smaller patterns of sound, rhythm, and meaning. In choosing their words poets strive for vividness, precision, and economy and give considerable attention to the pace and flow of words bound together in sentences. No sound, no word, no phrase is in itself poetic; it is the way they all work together that makes poetry. Because poetry is so complex and systematic, it is the most highly developed form of linguistic communication, difficult even for adults to fully comprehend.

At the same time, poetry is basically an oral art, and teachers can best serve their students by teaching it that way. Long before poems were written to be read, they were conceived to be recited to a group of listeners. A poem had to make a strong and instantaneous impact on the ears, senses, and emotions of its audience before any deep meanings were absorbed. Today, sophisticated readers of poetry are able to recreate this aural experience in their minds as they read alone silently. However, inexperienced children, reading a poem for the first time, and perhaps concentrating on decoding unfamiliar words, cannot make this kind of transformation. They need to hear poems spoken aloud with their aural characteristics emphasized.

I suggest that you introduce poems by reading or reciting them to the class without showing students the written texts. You should repeat a new poem as many times as children want to hear it, inviting them to join in when they can. When children know a poem well, it is time to offer them a written copy to use as they wish. A few children will have memorized the poem just through repetition, and some may choose to do that now. Still others will enjoy just rereading it to themselves or friends and family. If children really like a poem, you will not have to urge them to keep a copy for future reference.

Selecting the right poetry is important. You want quality, of course, but that doesn't mean you should introduce kindergartners to Shakespeare. In the primary grades, teachers should choose poems that are appealing in their content, simple in their language, pronounced in their rhythm, and strong in their use of alliteration and other sound devices. Students in the intermediate grades will like humorous poems and poems that tell stories. With middle schoolers who have grown up on poetry, teachers can try short modern poems that evoke strong feelings or visual images, classic story poems, and even some of Shakespeare's lighter pieces. Consider using such poems as "Portrait" by E. E. Cummings, "The Eve of St. Agnes" by John Keats, and "Winter" and "Spring" by William Shakespeare (both from *Love's Labors Lost*). To help you select other poems suitable for children of different ages, I offer a list of good poetry books at the end of this book.

Building a Poetic Repertoire

To enable students to build a repertoire of poetry, teachers need to introduce new poems every week and return to old favorites. In the primary grades an average of three poems a week is the ideal; two a week seems right for the intermediate grades, and one a week in middle school. With such a rapid rate of introduction, you cannot go over each poem as thoroughly as I've described, but that is not always necessary. Your students' initial reaction to a poem will let you know whether or not they want to make it their own. Classrooms at all grade levels should have collections of poetry in the classroom library, including poetry students learned in earlier grades. Copies of all the poems introduced in a grade should be placed in a class poetry book so students can find them again easily. At the same time, teachers should show students which published books poems came from and let them know if there are other poems by the same poet or poems on the same topics in the classroom collection. We want to encourage students to seek out their own poems by making quantity and variety available. In addition, students can construct their personal poetry collections in a loose-leaf notebook. Many students will want to illustrate the poems they like best or write them in fancy script. As their familiarity and understanding of poetry grow, students can add and delete poems, making their collections represent their specific tastes. When students write their own poems, they can add them to their collections, too.

While learning new poems and collecting their favorites, students can begin to try their hands at oral interpretation. Learning to read or recite poetry aloud is a source of joy and pride for most students. For their teachers it is a good way to informally assess reception, processing, storage, and production of a specialized form of language. When you understand the meaning of a poem and the sound qualities that support its meaning, you can read a poem so that others understand and enjoy it, too. The problem for most inexperienced poetry readers is that they follow the arrangement of words on the page and the rhythm pattern in the first line of a poem, when they should let the meaning, intent, and punctuation guide their reading.

In reading most poems, students should use the natural tones, pauses, and inflections of ordinary speech. They don't have to pay special attention to rhyme or alliteration or rhythm; those qualities will come through in a sensible oral reading. Yet there are important exceptions to this rule of thumb. When rhythm is the main feature of a poem, carrying its meaning, readers ought to emphasize it. Edgar Allan Poe's poem "The Bells" is an example. You are meant to hear the rhythmic clanging of the bells through the reader's voice. Many poems also have parts that were written to be read fast, quietly, dramatically, or angrily, because they are describing action that has that particular quality. For example, in reading the highly dramatic poem, "The Pied Piper of Hamlin," (Robert Browning) one would certainly not read the following lines in a casual tone and at normal speed:

> **Rats!**
> They fought the dogs and killed the cats,
> And bit the babies in the cradles.
> And ate the cheeses out of the vats
> And licked the soup from the cooks' own ladles,
> Split open the kegs of salted sprats,
> Made nests inside men's Sunday hats,
> And even spoiled the women's chats
> By drowning their speaking
> With shrieking and squeaking
> In fifty different sharps and flats.

In addition, many lighthearted poems, limericks, and nursery rhymes call for a humorous, sing-song delivery. Normal speech phrasing would destroy the fun of "Hey, diddle diddle, the cat and the fiddle . . ."

As you can see, to be able to read poetry aloud a reader needs to make prior decisions about the meaning, purpose, and mood of a poem. I suggest that you use small groups for guiding the oral interpretation of poetry, just as you use them for understanding books. The teacher's role in poetry groups is much the same as it is with prose literature groups: modeling, questioning, and encouraging the expression of different ideas and points of view. Because the language of poetry is often inverted or elliptical—and sometimes archaic—it may be hard for students to figure out sentences. And because poetry often uses figurative language to suggest an object or an event, students may have trouble figuring out what is being described. You can make things easier by paraphrasing lines that students are having trouble with and asking students to paraphrase other lines before reading them aloud.

It is also helpful to ask students to summarize the action of a poem, just as they would the plot of a story. If students continue to have difficulty in understanding what a poem says, it is likely that the poem's language is too sophisticated for their linguistic competence. You can find many poems written in appropriate language that communicate straightforward messages.

Although the study of poetry is done in groups, the preparation for an oral reading is an individual endeavor. Not everyone who studies a poem in a group is going to want to read or recite it to an audience. Those who do will need to practice on their own and try out their interpretations on a partner or two. They need to know what their partners get and do not get from their delivery:

Were all the words clear?

Were you distracted by anything I did?

How did the poem make you feel?

What did the poem mean to you?

After rehearsal and consultation, the reader will be ready for presentation to an audience. The size and composition of that audience should be what the reader feels comfortable with. It may be the poetry group, the whole class, another class, or a mixed audience. One teacher I know plans an annual poetry reading show for parents, in which all students participate, each one reading or reciting one poem they have come to love that year.

Many of the poems teachers or students present orally serve well as the foundation for writing original poems. In my opinion, novice poets need concrete models for writing poetry. Their sense of what goes into a poem, picked up through reading, listening, and discussion, is not enough to guide or support them in trying to create the complex patterns of poetry. Lacking experience, students cannot wield the tools of rhyme, alliteration, consonance, assonance, imagery, and refrains all at once as poets do so skillfully. In fact, outside of rhyme, most students are not even aware that such tools exist because poets blend them so subtly into the whole design of their poems.

In the beginning, a poetic model is just a form to be imitated. For instance, young children who have become familiar with the poem "The Little Turtle," by Vachel Lindsay, quoted below, can be asked to use it as a model for writing their own poems about other animals with other adventures. Although formal analysis of poetry is not an appropriate activity for elementary or middle school students, learning to recognize and appreciate the most common features of poetry is within their grasp, and necessary if they are going to write poems of their own. With this poem, primary grade children need to notice which lines rhyme and how many metric feet (accented and unaccented syllables) there are in each line. These are the poetic devices or tools that they should try to use when they create their own poems. Here is Lindsay's poem:

> There was a little turtle.
> He lived in a box.
> He swam in a puddle.
> He climbed on the rocks.
>
> He snapped at a mosquito.
> He snapped at a flea.
> He snapped at a minnow.
> And he snapped at me.
>
> He caught the mosquito.
> He caught the flea.
> He caught the minnow.
> But he didn't catch me.

There was a little skunk.
He lived in a cave.
He swam in a lake.
He was very brave.

He sprayed at a chipmunk.
He sprayed at a bee.
He sprayed at a bird.
And he sprayed at me!

He caught the chipmunk.
He caught the bee.
He caught the bird
But he didn't catch me.
                    —*Sachi Komai*

Is this good poetry? No. It is not even very original. For the most part, Sachi used the model as presented and substituted a few words. On the other hand, her substitutions were not random. She took care to duplicate the pattern of action in the original, and she found sensible rhymes for her lines. Her poem also shows an awareness of meter and some effort to reproduce it, although she hasn't fully grasped the difference between words and syllables. What she was trying to do was to juggle meaning, sound, and rhythm all at once. Not bad for a second grader.

As students become familiar with many poems and their various patterns of sound and rhythm, they grow more skillful in using patterns without mimicking them. Following are two poems by fifth-grade students written on a model that used the color orange as a metaphor for feelings.

Tan is a potato
A dirty shoe
A desktop
A cork
And a tea bag, too.
Piecrust
and mountain dust
Both are tan,

Cardboard,
Paper bags
And the gingerbread man.
And in the morning when you wake up,
Tan is the smell
In your coffee cup.
—*Erin Brathwaite*

Gray is a rain cloud,
A loaf of stale bread,
Smoke
And ashes
A day that you dread.
Tin cans
And trash cans
Are gray,
Wads of gum, too,
Cold potatoes,
Fog
And a worn-out tennis shoe.
The feeling of gray is sad
Like a drizzly day,
When nobody has
Anything "right" to say.
—*Scott Esser*

Not only were these student poets able to keep the form and the spirit of the original, they also included quite a bit of sensible, unobtrusive rhyme. Scott also did a good job of maintaining the same dull, sad mood throughout. Erin, on the other hand, inserted a few bright objects in her overall description of dull things.

The next examples of children's poetry I want to give are probably the best I have available. After reading William Carlos Williams' poem "This Is Just to Say," a group of fifth graders wrote their own apologies. Like the original, their poems reflect minor transgressions against a friend or family member about which they are only mildly regretful. While retaining the spirit of the model, however, the poets have moved quite a distance away from it, finding their own topics, forms, and tones. Here is

> I have eaten
> the plums
> that were in
> the icebox
> and which you were probably
> saving for breakfast
>
> Forgive me
> they were delicious
> so sweet
> and so cold

And here are the students' poems:

> I have broken
> your favorite china glasses.
> I know you're having your boss over tonight,
>
> and if you don't
> impress him you will
> probably
> lose your job.
>
> Forgive me. I thought
> the plastic cups and the
> lobster looked fine.
>   *—Katy Kamps*

> Jennifer,
> your two yellow lollipops
> looked so delicious.
>
> I promised
> in writing
> to get you
> another one
> if you'd
> give me one.

Forgive me
for tricking you.
I put the note
in the garbage
after you gave me
the lollipop.
—*Renee Jarrett*

Incidentally, this type of poem breaks the rule of thumb I mentioned earlier: following punctuation and normal speech phrasing when reading a poem aloud. In these examples, the lines suggest a slow, interrupted reading; perhaps the poem's narrator is trying to think of what to say. These poems should be read with slight pauses after each line.

Although I have emphasized using models for writing poetry throughout this section, I don't want to leave you with the impression that students shouldn't be allowed to go off on their own and write without models. When students know lots of poems and understand how they work, many will want to try something totally original and will be able to produce excellent work. In my own collection of students' poetry, there are many such examples. As a teacher, I would never discourage a child from writing a poem, and I would always give that child my full attention and support. The general line of advice given in this chapter is based on my belief that writing poetry is the hardest thing we ask children to do and, thus, needs a lot of support. It is also based on a common theory of teaching: Showing is always better than telling.

I will end this chapter with a vignette of a teacher and her combined grade four/five class working on a very free form of poetry: poetic monologues (see page 103). They did not use a specific model in this instance because they had been writing poetry for a long time and had internalized many of its characteristics. I think that their poems display their knowledge of poetry and their ability to use it to differentiate their learning.

References

Koch, K. 1973. *Rose, Where Did You Get That Red?: Teaching Great Poetry to Children.* New York: Random House.

Larrick, N. 1971. *Somebody Turned on the Tap in These Kids: Poetry and Young People Today.* New York: Delacorte Press.

Writing Poetic Monologues

Arlys Caslavka started her fourth and fifth graders thinking about the problems common among children their age. It often seems that they are being bossed by everyone, denied their own preferences, and forced to do things they do not want to do. Several children recall such situations: having to eat food they didn't like; having to baby-sit when they had something important to do; being laughed at; being left out. Others agree that similar things have happened to them and that the problems seem universal.

Ms. Caslavka suggests that they express their feelings in poetry in the style of a monologue—that is, by giving the child's side of a two-way conversation. She demonstrates orally, recalling an incident from her own childhood, and the children realize that they can figure out what the unheard person is saying from listening to her side of the story alone. They decide on situations of their own and start their poems.

As the children write, Ms. Caslavka spends time helping individuals. Out of habit, the children want to make their poems literary, so she has to keep asking, "Is that what you would say?" When the children give a good oral response, she tells them to write it down just that way. Another strategy she encourages them to use is reading their poems aloud to a classmate.

The second problem is with phrasing—where to stop the lines. Ms. Caslavka advises children to imagine the natural silences and the pauses where the other person is speaking; the writers can use them as signals to end a line. There is much rewriting, much conferring with the teacher and classmates. In the end, the children love the results. Despite the ordinary situations and everyday language, their works seem more like real poetry than anything else they have written this year.

Hand Me Down
But it's not in style!
I don't like the color.
And also it doesn't go with my shoes.
But Mom, I don't like them.
Do I have to wear them?
Why always hand me downs?
Can't I ever get anything new?
I don't want to wear Lisa's old pants.

— ALLIE KUNES

The Deadly Doctor
What! Take off all my clothes? NO WAY?
Mom, what is he going to do?
Ooo, that's cold on my back.
Can I hear your heart now?
What made my leg jump like that?
That's a weird feeling on my knee!
Mom, you said he wasn't going to give me a shot!
Where's the nearest elevator!
Oh, doctor, let me go!

— JON MCFERREN

The Water
I don't feel like going in right now.
Do I have to?
No, I'm not afraid to.
Do sharks swim in this lake?
Just asking.
You said it wasn't cold, Mom.
It's getting deeper.
It's up to my knees.
Now it's up to my tummy.
How far are we going?
        SPLASH!
No, it wasn't too bad.
Let's stay longer, 'kay, Mom?

— PETER O'NEIL

Terrible Tasting Tomato Juice
I don't like it.
I hate it.
I won't drink it!
If I do, I'll throw up.
Maybe even die!
Mom, last night I could have . . .
Well, never mind.
I tried to give it to the dog,
And he wouldn't drink it.
Neither would the goldfish.
Next day they were floating on the top.
So Mom, I'm not drinking it either.

— KRISTIN OLSON

8

Learning Comes Alive with Projects

In elementary and middle school classrooms, literacy learning is not confined to the language arts curriculum. As we have seen in previous chapters, lessons that are primarily designed to teach history, science, or some other school subject often involve receiving, in-processing, storing, out-processing, and producing new language products with new concepts and new vocabulary. The social context of the classroom also pushes students to expand the range of their language competence through such activities as writing classroom rules, reading the daily newspaper, and role playing to resolve playground disputes. Even within the language arts program, reading, writing, and speaking are not practiced for their own sake, but to support the study of content, as when students are asked to report on the life of an author or research the history of nursery rhymes. In this chapter I will focus on student projects in various subject matter areas that also offer new and interesting opportunities for differentiating literacy learning.

A project, as I am using the term, is a multifaceted and polished piece of work that demonstrates high-level learning. Typically, it combines skills and information from various sources and takes some time to complete. Although a project could be a piece of writing, it is more likely to be a physical display that includes more than just one item rendered in one mode. For example, a play written and performed by students would be more commonly considered a project than a play script alone.

Projects are an important aspect of differentiated instruction. Not only do projects allow students to follow their interests and imaginations, they also encourage students to apply academic learning to real problems and produce something of real-world value. In addition, projects provide an opportunity for all students to shine. With projects, those who are not talented writers or voracious readers may give center stage to their strengths in other areas.

While lauding the benefits of projects, I must acknowledge that they can also be tricky business for students and teachers to manage. And projects can be a frustrating experience for parents whose children delay working on them until the night before they are due. Unfortunately, last-minute panics at home are a common experience, not because students are lazy, but because there has been inadequate preparation and guidance in the classroom for them to carry out the projects on their own.

Preparing for Projects

Projects need to begin with preparation, not assignments. Before launching into a project, you have to prepare yourself, your students, and the classroom for the work ahead. All the following steps should be covered, though not necessarily in the order they are given.

1. **Decide the type of project.**
   Which types of projects are most likely to lead to integration of knowledge and skills, and produce growth?
   Which type is most appropriate for the topic studied: a report, poster, construction, dramatization, or a piece of artwork?
   Will project topics be assigned, open to choice, or completely free?

2. **Determine if students have the general skills to do this type of project.**
   Can they find the information they will need in reference sources?
   Are they able to judge their own capabilities ahead of time and choose a project they can complete successfully?
   Do they know how to conduct and record an interview?
   Will they be able to manage the tools and materials needed?
   Can they make detailed plans and keep records?

3. **Plan to teach the specialized skills and information students will need.**
   Are there new processes that students will have to learn?
   Is there unfamiliar vocabulary and/or content?

Is the project so unfamiliar and demanding that you will have to lead students through it, or is it simple enough for them to do most of the work on their own?

4. **Make a schedule for beginning and ending the projects.**
    Tailor the length of the project to the attention span of the students.
    Allow time and space for part of the work to be done at school.
    Figure out how to fit in time for individual guidance.

5. **Figure out what materials and tools, in what quantity, students will need.**
    Can the project be done with cheap or homemade materials?
    How will you make tools and materials accessible to everyone?
    Will you allow tools to go home and, if so, how will you be sure you get them back?

As you can see, a lot of bases have to be covered in preparation for projects. For this reason, I suggest that teachers delay projects until well into the school year when they know their students' strengths and weaknesses and, then, that they make projects the culminating activity of a thoroughly taught unit. By the same logic, I advise teachers to circumscribe students' choices of projects rather than give them free rein. I have seen too many students who, in their initial enthusiasm, have bitten off more than they could chew. And I have seen too many teachers drive themselves to the brink of a meltdown by trying to guide thirty students of widely varying abilities through the process of producing thirty diverse projects.

Two Approaches to Projects in Middle School

Let me give two true examples of what can happen in a classroom when projects are approached differently. In one classroom all students were expected to do the same project. In the other they were allowed to choose almost any topic, as long as it could be explored through a certain type of project.

In the first instance, a middle school teacher decided to culminate the year's study of mathematics by having every student draw a scale design of a house plan and simulate obtaining a mortgage, buying furniture, and contracting for landscaping. Within this uniform assignment, the teacher provided for differentiation by asking students to invent fictional identities for themselves and create fictional families. However, before allowing the students to get started, she warned them that their family's characteristics (e.g., numbers and genders of children) would impose certain conditions on their house designs and gave examples. Then she assigned each family a job (or jobs), a yearly income, an amount for savings on hand, and a mortgage limit based on income. She believed this step was necessary because most students would probably have chosen glamorous jobs with large salaries for themselves, thereby making it easy to have anything they wanted in their houses; and she wanted to simplify the project for students with limited math skills and make it more challenging for the math whizzes in the class. Working within the parameters of family needs and income limits, students had to make decisions about the size of their house, the number of bedrooms and bathrooms, and whether they could afford such things as an exercise room or a family entertainment center. At the same time, they were free to choose the styles of architecture and furniture and the color schemes they preferred, and to skimp on some things in one place to have luxuries in another. For example, they could buy a cheaper lot and put a fancier house on it. I viewed all these projects when they were finished, and though they varied in complexity and artistry, all showed considerable thought, hard work, and an acceptable level of quality. Many of them were quite original, despite the restrictions imposed.

In the second situation, another middle school teacher also wanted to culminate math study with projects. To start things off, she gave every student a million imaginary dollars to design and run a nonprofit enterprise for one year. She showed the class some projects from past years and explained the kinds of things money needed to be spent on, such as the purchase or rental of a building, salaries, and supplies. The students' job was to select a venture they were interested in, research it, describe it, and figure out how to spend the million dollars. One student created a horse farm, another a house for homeless teens, and another built a large sailboat on which to take friends on a yearlong cruise. Other projects were equally diverse. When I saw the finished projects and heard the students' oral presentations, I could appreciate the work they had done and the amount of individual help the teacher had given, but I felt that the resulting projects were far removed from reality. It seemed to me that students had no real understanding of the components of their projects or what those components might cost. I suspect that both the students and their teacher were overwhelmed with the amount of research that had to be done to get information about costs and materials and wound up making wild estimates.

In both of these instances, teachers had covered the necessary preparation. Most of the project work was done in the classrooms under teacher guidance, and with step-by-step plans that the teachers directed. At the appropriate times in the process, both teachers gave lessons on different aspects of finance that helped the students to figure out costs. They also met with students individually. One important difference, however, was that the first teacher was able to give whole-class lessons about drawing to scale; the average sizes of houses and rooms; the appliances, furniture, and decorations houses usually have; and other details that students might not think of on their own. The second teacher had to gather much more information over a broader territory and give it to students individually or in very small groups. While I consider both approaches legitimate, I feel that the second is too cumbersome and requires much more effort from the teacher, the students, and probably the parents than could be justified by its results.

Perhaps the best approach would have been some middle ground between these two examples—one where students were given more choices, but where there were similarities among choices. For example, in the second classroom the project process could have been simplified and unified by asking students to design a public service facility that would provide homeless people with only one service: food, shelter, medical care, or job training. Then it would have been much easier for the students and the teacher to figure out the realistic needs of each project and the costs. Another change that would have simplified the work and produced better projects would be to have students work in small groups rather than alone. There would have been a smaller number of projects, and the research for each could have been distributed among several students.

Project Planning and Production

Once the preparation has been completed and the assignment given, you need to help students plan their projects. First, it would be helpful to let students see some projects (or photos of them) from previous years. It would be even better to invite a few former students to come into the classroom to show their projects and explain how they planned and did the project work. Then, students—working alone or in small groups—could choose their projects. They would need to write a proposal (such as in Figure 8-1), describing what they intend to do, scheduling the work over the allotted time, and including a list of the tools and materials they think they will need. Using this proposal device is important in helping students comprehend the types and amount of work that lie ahead and in allowing the teacher to see if students' choices of projects and work plans are reasonable.

> Project Proposal
>
> Names of Group Members: Date 4/17
>   Sally G, Jeremy Y, Bruce D   Grade 6
>   Helen K, Laura S, Dan J.
>
> Title of Project: The Great Wall of China
>
> Description We will produce a book about the
>   Great Wall of China. We will include information
>   about when and how it was built and what
>   it is like today
>
> Time Plan:
> Week 1. Read all the books and articles we can
>   find. Take notes.
>
> Week 2. Plan all the reports and pictures to
>   go into it.
>
> Week 3 Write the reports and draw the
>   pictures.
>
> Week 4 Put the book together and present
>   our project to the class
> Materials Needed:
>   Paper, paints, cardboard

FIGURE 8-1: *Project Proposal*

In the outline for project preparation I indicated that some work on projects should be done at school. Just how much depends on the capabilities of the students and the complexities of project. But whatever you decide on the matter, I think that the central core of any project should be kept at school throughout. Projects tend to be large in size and awkward to transport—especially on a school bus. Let students do some writing, reading, and drawing at home while the base of the project remains in the classroom.

As students work on their projects, you will need to monitor their progress. Depending on the age and competence of the class and the time allotted for the project, two or three progress checks may be necessary. Set up a form with spaces to be filled in, something like the one in Figures 8-2a and 8-2b. Not only will this device make monitoring easier for the teacher, it will get students into the habit of self-monitoring, which is a necessary component of differentiated learning.

Reading these forms and doing a quick visual survey of the incomplete projects on hand will tell you who needs help and what kind. On this basis you can schedule conferences with those individuals or groups who are lagging behind or mired in problems. Changes in projects—usually simplifications—can also be negotiated during a conference.

The final step is planning for project presentation. I didn't include this step earlier as a part of the preliminary planning because I think students are not ready to make a decision until they see how their projects are turning

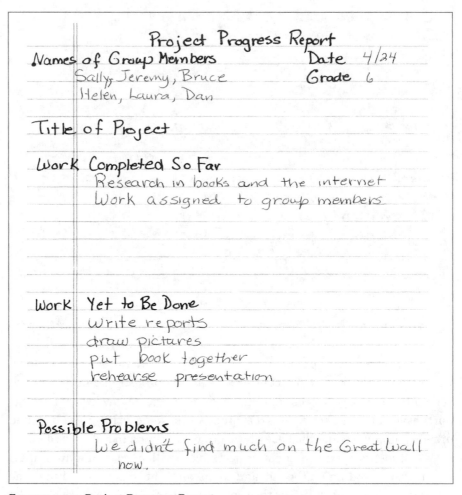

FIGURE 8-2A: *Project Progress Report*

Project Progress Report

Title of Project

Names of Designers

Work Completed So Far
(with dates and initials of contributing workers)

Work Yet to Be Done
(with dates of proposed completion and initials of workers assigned to each task)

Possible Problems

out. Now, with projects almost completed, they are better able to judge if they should be shared among themselves, with other classes, or with parents. Since a presentation almost inevitably involves speaking to an audience, this too needs to be planned and practiced in advance. Speeches are one part of a project that can be worked on extensively at home because family members are in a good position to tell children if what they plan to say is audible, clear, and interesting. Families should also ask questions of the presenter as a kind of warm-up for any questions audience members might ask.

The presentation of projects to an audience is an occasion for celebration. Refreshments, dressing up, and perhaps programs are in order. Make it a point to take photographs, too—some from a distance—of the project and its designer(s), and at least one close-up, showing the details of the project. Give one set of photos to each student as a souvenir, and keep one set to show subsequent classes when they start their projects. The projects themselves go home with students. If they survive for a year, you can ask some former students to bring them back to school to show next year's class.

In this long discussion of projects, I've given scant attention to the two things this book is about: differentiated learning and literacy. Although I've assumed that readers could see those things lurking between the lines, I owe you some explicit discussion of the roles differentiation and literacy play. By definition, all projects represent differentiated learning. Even when the type and topic of a project is prescribed, students demonstrate their knowledge and skills in different ways and to different extents. There is also the element of personal interpretation in a project, which, in reality, is the product component of the learning process described in earlier chapters. The information a student receives, how he processes that information, stores it, and then expresses it in a product make up his unique interpretation of what is interesting and important in all that he has learned. Above all, that is what projects show us about student learning.

At the same time it is impossible to produce a project without using sophisticated forms of spoken and written language. Students have to read and write to get the information they need, they have to consult with adults and classmates about carrying out the phases of their projects, and they have to write and speak to communicate the meaning of their projects to others. Since projects differ so much in type and topic, it is difficult to be more specific. What I can do, however, is to present a list of literacy tasks that are typical parts of projects. As you consider particular projects, these tasks are likely to be involved.

Writing a project proposal

Composing a questionnaire to get information

Interviewing people who know a lot about the topic of a project

Writing, practicing, and giving speeches for a project presentation

Making telephone calls requesting information

Writing letters asking for information or samples

Making posters advertising the project presentation

Talking about planning and progress during group meetings

Conferring with the teacher about problems

Writing captions for photographs and drawings

Reading sections in textbooks, magazines, and reference books

Reading directions for using tools and materials

Writing, reading, practicing, and performing play scripts

Proofreading headings and captions for posters

Writing a progress report

Recording information from reading or interviewing

Reading explanatory information from other people's projects

Searching catalogues and newspaper ads to find costs of materials

To illustrate differentiated learning and literacy involvement further, I will end this chapter with two vignettes of students working on projects. Since the examples given at the beginning of the chapter were taken from middle school classrooms, I've chosen these vignettes to show what younger children can do. Because of their limited experience and fewer independent work skills, their projects are shorter and simpler than the ones already described, and the processes of planning and production are quite teacher-directed. Yet you will see in these children's projects considerable evidence of literacy competence and differentiated learning.

Programming a Robot

Several weeks into the semester, Harriet Gorski's third graders decide to design and program robots to do some ordinary home and classroom jobs. Having written job descriptions for classroom management and worked with simple computer programs, they are confident that they can apply their skills to this new challenge. Once they plunge into the task, however, they are not so sure. They are having trouble writing the programs.

In class discussion, two problems emerge:

1. Some of the jobs they have chosen are really too complicated and ambiguous to be programmed. Going to the store, for example, involves possible unforeseen circumstances and decisions that a robot cannot make.
2. Other jobs have not been broken down into their composite steps. The students cannot just tell a robot to "dry the dishes."

To help solve the problems, the class will try role playing, with a child acting as a robot and the others giving commands. Each "robot" is to do exactly as it is told and to say "error" if the command is not perfectly clear. Robots are cautioned not to help the programmers by doing the right thing when they have not been told to.

First, the children try a table-setting task with Helen acting as the robot and three children alternating commands. "Pick up the placemat." She does so. "Put it on the table." She puts it in the middle at a slant. "No, put it two inches from the edge facing you." She does it and the programmers are pleased. Put the plate in the middle of the mat." Again, success. "Put the fork next to the plate." She puts it to the right. The programmers are catching on and quickly correct themselves. "Put it to the left, one inch from the plate." Commands continue, with small missteps but no major breakdown,

and finally one place is set. Since they want four places, the final command is "Go back to 10 and repeat three times." Helen starts to obey by putting the second place setting on top of the first. There is some consultation while the programmers decide how to correct her. They decide to add the command, "Move right to the next side of the table" and then "Go back to 10."

After role playing is done by several groups, all the children have a better idea of what tasks are suitable and how precise their commands must be. Working individually, they now create their robots and write their programs. Below is one child's program for a robot to make his bed.

Design a Robot to Do a Job

The Job: Make my bed for me when it is messed up.

Here is the program step by step:

```
10   Tuck the sheet under the mattress.
20   Pick up the blanket.
30   Lay the blanket on the bed.
40   Flatten until no wrinkles.
50   Are there any wrinkles left?
60   If there are wrinkles go to 40.
70   If there are no wrinkles go to 80.
80   Pick up the quilt.
90   Lay on the bed.
100  Flatten until no wrinkles.
110  If there are any wrinkles, go to 100.
120  If there are no wrinkles go to 130.
130  Put the pillow on the head of the bed.
140  Say "I'm done" and I'll check it.
150  If I say it doesn't look right go to 10.
160  If I say it looks fine, take a rest.
170  End
```

— Terry Miles

Helping to Save the Penguins

For a small group of Marlys Sloup's fourth graders, reading the book *Mr. Popper's Penguins* by Richard Atwater has led to an extensive project in persuasion. During the reading Mrs. Sloup made nonfiction resources available so that the children could learn as much as possible about penguins. By coincidence, one of their classroom magazines also had an article on penguins. The children read that the French government is constructing an airstrip in Antarctica that threatens the access of Emperor penguins to their breeding grounds and is destroying the nesting sites of a larger number of Adelie penguins. Always concerned for wildlife, the children and their teacher are particularly touched by the plight of these appealing birds, whose lifestyle seems so precarious in this industrial age. Picking up on a suggestion at the end of the article, they write a group letter to the Antarctica Project for further information.

The brochures they receive in reply contain several suggestions of things concerned people can do to help. The children choose to circulate a petition asking the Antarctic Treaty governments and the United Nations to declare Antarctica a World Park.

They discuss the most effective way to do this.

Colin proposes that they set up a table in the lunchroom with pictures and reading material, but the others protest that no one will have the time to come over. The kids are in too much of a hurry to get out on the playground. "Then, let's go to the class-rooms," he counters.

"Okay, but the little kids won't understand," says Shelley. "We have to do more."

"Why don't we make some signs and carry them around out on the playground," David suggests. "Then everyone will want to know what it's all about, but we won't tell them. We'll just say, 'Wait 'til next week.'"

Mrs. Sloup helps the children to plan signs that will be both informative and provocative. Then, she divides the explanation into a four-part presentation that explains and makes a plea for support. The children write their parts using the brochures they received from the Antarctica Project, then rehearse them in front of their own class. Four of the children will give the formal presentation while the other two will answer questions. After five days they are ready and will start the sign-carrying part of their project tomorrow.

References

ALLEN, R. R., K. L. BROWN, AND J. YATVIN. 1986. *Learning Language Through Communication: A Functional Perspective.* Belmont, CA: Wadsworth.

PERSONKE, C. R., AND D. JOHNSON. 1987. *Language Arts Instruction and the Beginning Teacher: A Practical Guide.* Englewood Cliffs, NJ: Prentice Hall.

Making Room for Exceptional Students

For both philosophical and financial reasons most schools today include gifted students and students with disabilities in regular classrooms for the major portion of the school day. Parents and administrators want these exceptional students to have the social benefits of being with their peers, and they want classroom teachers to provide appropriate learning activities for them, too. Although most teachers agree in principle, they recognize that policies of inclusion do not always come with the plans and resources to make them work. Differentiating instruction for students at the extremes of academic performance often means that teachers are expected to plan special curricula for them, use different texts, and teach them separately from the rest of the class. With class sizes already bigger than they should be; with standards and tests demanding higher-level learning from all students; and with human and material resources for classrooms at an all-time low; how can teachers do still more? How can they serve their exceptional students without depriving the rest of their students of the teaching and support they are entitled to?

Inclusion of Exceptional Students

The short answer to both questions is: They can't. "Twenty-four-seven" is as far as any teacher can go, and that's not far enough to meet the expectations described above. But there is also a long answer that this chapter will examine. That answer is based on two idealistic, yet pragmatic and equitable, principles.

1. Exceptional students are members of the classroom community, who should be working with, learning from, teaching, and socializing with others as equals.

2. There is room within a good classroom curriculum for exceptional students to pursue their interests and work at their own level of difficulty.

In practical terms, these principles mean that teachers have to find ways for exceptional students to "fit in" socially and academically, rather than trying to create separate programs for them. Such students should participate in class units, lessons, routines, and rituals; collaborate with classmates in small-group activities and partnerships; and work on projects and tasks; all to the limits of their abilities. They should receive help from adults and classmates when they need it, and give help in return when they are able to do so.

Working with Disabled Students

You may be thinking that what I have just asserted is reasonable enough for gifted students but way beyond the capabilities of the disabled. If you have in mind severely mentally handicapped students, you may be right. But I assume, according to law, that when such students are included in classrooms they are accompanied by aides who have been trained to work with them on programs planned by the specialists who have the primary responsibility for their education. When these students are capable of participating in class activities, they should participate; when they are not, aides must oversee their work and behavior.

For our purposes, let's consider the situations of mildly to moderately disabled children who—seemingly in increasing numbers—populate our schools. It is not unusual for from one to six such students to be assigned to an elementary or middle school classroom, without any extra aides, and with only brief periods of instruction from a specialist. The classroom teacher has the major responsibility for these disabled children.

Ideally, you will know beforehand that such students are coming and have time to learn about them and prepare. First, you will need to study school records to find out their academic levels and their successes and problems from the past. Then, you should talk to people who know the

1. study record

2. talk to people

3. Talk to Student

4. Administer a test

children: former teachers, parents, and diagnostic specialists or thera-pists. You will want to talk to the children, too, to see how they feel about school, schoolwork, teachers, and classmates. Before the school year starts, it would be a good idea to administer one or two of the informal assessments described in Chapter 3 to get a better handle on how students might perform with various tasks. Using all these sources, you should be able to get answers to the following questions about each disabled student:

1. How well does the student work with a small group, a partner, on his/her own?

2. How long is his/her attention span for various types of activities?

3. How does the student behave when not under direct supervision of the teacher?

4. Is the student able to make friends among classmates?

5. What are the student's social strengths and weaknesses?

6. Is the student likely to become aggressive, withdrawn, or emotional in class, and, if so, under what circumstances?

7. What are the student's special talents or interests?

Creating Student Profiles

With the information you have gathered, you can develop a profile for each disabled student in relation to the class curriculum, organizational struc-tures, routines, and behavioral expectations. These profiles need not be lengthy or detailed. Their purpose is to synthesize in the teacher's mind what to expect from students and how to modify work appropriately. At first, you will probably have to refer to the written profiles when doing weekly or daily planning, but soon you will know the children well enough to note automatically when modifications are needed. The following are examples of three profiles a teacher might write. They describe fictitious students, but incorporate the literacy characteristics of students who failed the Washington state reading test in 1999, as described in a recent study by Marsha Buly and Sheila Valencia.

Lisa is a sociable sixth grader of average intelligence with disabilities in reading and writing. Although her oral reading is fast and error free, her comprehension is poor. Her writing is disorganized, with shallow content and immature vocabulary. She performs adequately in classroom activities that do not require much reading or background knowledge, but she does poorly when expected to distinguish between facts and opinions. When it comes to group planning of events or projects, Lisa is a strong team member. She shows enthusiasm and practical skills. Lisa's interests are almost exclusively physical and social. She does not appear to be intellectually curious. She takes gymnastics and swimming classes outside of school and plays on the school soccer team. Her heroes are women athletes. She tends to think of schoolwork as something you have to put up with in order to enjoy the benefits of team sports and social relationships.

Paul, a third grader who has above-average intelligence, is disabled in reading. His decoding is slow and labored. Although he knows the common sounds associated with letters, he has difficulty blending them into words. When not reminded specifically to decode unfamiliar words, he uses the beginning sounds and the surrounding context to guess at them. Nevertheless, he can retell the plot of a story with fair accuracy, leaving out only some details. In his writing, content, word choice, and organization are good, but poor spelling and run-on sentences make his pieces hard to read. He spells words as they sound to him, not according to rules. Paul has extensive knowledge of science, which is his major interest. He excels in science discussions and projects, but is somewhat passive in most other activities. Although Paul usually draws in his notebook during whole-class explanations, he is able to remember the information given. Paul says he likes school and his teachers, but he wishes that more of the work was interesting. He has only two friends in the class, boys with similar interests.

Janie is a second grader of average intelligence who can read only picture books with one or two lines of text. Even then, it appears that she has memorized the sentences. Both her decoding and comprehension are at kindergarten level. Janie has had instruction in phonemic awareness and systematic phonics, but she cannot remember what has been taught from one day to the next. The rules of phonics seem to confuse her more than they help her. Her writing is very immature both in content and mechanical features. She is shy and does not speak much in class or in private conversation. On the playground, she associates with younger children. In the classroom she seeks out the more motherly girls who often do much of her work for her.

*services of
Tutor for
comprehension*

Planning Modifications

Both Lisa and Paul have enough strengths to function in a grade-level curriculum while they are working to improve their literacy competence. In different ways, both would benefit from regularly using the "Read, Talk, and Write" strategy, described in Chapter 4, when they are assigned to read textbooks or other informational material. This strategy would help Lisa improve her comprehension, vocabulary, and writing. Paul would be helped to get the details he misses when he reads alone. Lisa, in addition, needs individual tutoring in comprehension from a specialist. In the classroom, she can also profit from being included in a reading group where comprehension is emphasized. There she would have opportunities to generate questions about books and to summarize sections orally. Since Lisa's performance is likely to be weakest when she works alone, the teacher should try to have her work with a partner most of the time, ideally with a girl she admires. Lisa's reading partners should be instructed to model their own comprehension strategies for her. At the same time, her teacher needs to seek out reading materials that will appeal to Lisa: biographies of women athletes, sports magazines, and action stories. She can help Lisa build background knowledge through materials that have lots of pictures and only a little text. The teacher also needs to involve Lisa in projects that require her to do limited amounts of reading and writing for successful completion.

Paul, on the other hand, needs individual help with decoding and spelling. Learning to spell common prefixes and suffixes and how to attach them to word roots would be of benefit. He, too, can function in a grade-level group for reading and projects, but he will probably do better if he does not have to read full assignments. The teacher can have him read only parts of chapters and listen to the rest on tape. He should also be expected to listen carefully when others in his group are discussing sections he hasn't read. When it is Paul's turn to summarize a part of a book, he can be asked, "What else?" if his summary is sketchy. Paul should be partnered with students who can model decoding strategies for him when they come to unfamiliar words. Although Paul is capable of working on individual writing and projects, the teacher needs to monitor his work closely for accuracy and attention to details. The teacher can use Paul's science interest to get him involved in books about various branches of science and technology and science fiction novels that would broaden the scope of his interests. Paul might benefit from opportunities to present science information to classmates or younger children.

It is questionable whether Janie belongs in a second-grade classroom. She is socially and academically immature and appears to have missed out on a lot of the preschool language and literacy experiences children need. However, since Janie has been placed in a second-grade classroom, her teacher has no choice but to do everything she can to get her the extra help she needs to make significant progress. In terms of resources, Janie needs individual tutoring from a specialist in a Reading Recovery-type program and some assistance during class activities from an aide who will use the same Reading Recovery strategies. Janie also needs to take an active role in the class's oral language and literature activities to the fullest extent possible. She can participate in a reading group, too, by preparing short pieces of the text ahead of time and using audiotapes to hear the rest of stories. In the reading group Janie should be asked to retell sections that other students have read aloud. For recreational reading, Janie can be encouraged to reread books she has covered with the specialist. She can read them aloud to a partner and then to her parents at home. Because Janie is likely to have trouble with projects, she should work with a group and be assigned tasks that are within her grasp. On occasion, she should be invited to take a book she knows to the kindergarten and read it to a child there. For writing, Janie could dictate her ideas to the teacher or an aide, then recopy them into her notebook.

The Need for Extra Resources

In advocating for the inclusion of disabled students in classroom activities, I have also made clear that extra resources are needed to support them adequately. Lisa and Paul can probably do well with thirty to forty-five minutes of instruction from a reading specialist three times a week; Janie needs specialized tutoring every day and help from a trained aide. All three students need to have books in the classroom library that interest them and that they can read independently. All three also need a computer for writing and a tape recorder for listening to taped books. In addition, Janie could use some extra time in other literacy environments besides her own classroom—for example, the school library. Right now, it is more important for her to get the literacy experiences she has missed than to study science and social studies. Finally, all three children need a classroom role that gives them small responsibilities for reading and writing and lots of prestige. Under supervision, Lisa or Paul could learn how to be teacher assistants, putting diagrams and directions on transparencies, labeling materials, and writing homework assignments on the chalkboard.

They could also write short messages and reminders to the teacher as if they were her secretaries. Janie could learn to read labels in the classroom so she could put away and distribute supplies. She could also deliver mail to classmates and other teachers if she learned to recognize their names.

The Role of Specialists

In describing the needs of these three fictional children and suggesting how teachers might provide for them within the context of a regular literacy program, I have only touched on the possibilities. In consultation with the specialists who work with the children, teachers can develop other strategies and find other materials that are effective for classroom work. At the same time, all modifications and materials will be more effective if the specialist works alongside the teacher in the regular classroom. There are many reasons why pulling out students for special classes has shown little success over the years. The primary problem is that what is being taught in special classes is usually unrelated to what children are doing in their regular classrooms, so it isn't sufficiently practiced, and it doesn't transfer. Secondarily, the continuity of classroom instruction is interrupted for the child who is pulled out. If he is pulled out more than once a day—as many children are—it is destroyed. Finally, there is a stigma attached to being pulled out that no euphemism can erase. The child who goes out for "reading enrichment" thinks it is because he is dumb, and many of those who remain in the classroom think the same thing. They wonder what kind of black magic is going on in that special class to make those dumb kids smart again.

When specialists work in classrooms, in partnership with classroom teachers, the story is quite different. Both teachers plan together, aligning the special program with the classroom program. The specialist works with small groups at times and with individuals at other times, pulling nondisabled children into the activities. She teaches students strategies and processes that they can put to work right away. Everyone can see and hear what the specialist is doing (including the classroom teacher), and it looks like the same kind of work they are doing, only maybe more fun. If there is a downside, it is the less efficient use of the specialist's time. But that problem, too, can be addressed by grouping children with similar disabilities in the same classroom. Earlier I mentioned a middle school I visited where a learning disabilities specialist spends two hours in the morning in one teacher's classroom working with disabled students on language arts and social studies and two hours in the afternoon in another teacher's room working with the same students on math and science. In an elementary school in the same district, a specialist teams all day with a fifth-grade teacher who has eight learning disabled students in her classroom of thirty. She works not only with those eight students but also with any other students who need special help.

The Curriculum Factor

With careful planning, sensible modifications, and support, learning-disabled students can function successfully in their grade level classrooms. But in addition to the work of the specialist and the teacher, much depends on the classroom curriculum. Is it based on related themes and concepts or a disorderly heap of discrete skills and information? Learning-disabled children are not mentally retarded. They have the ability to grasp concepts that are presented in meaningful contexts, well explained and illustrated, and strengthened through repeated practice. Where they run into trouble is with lessons that require them to take in and remember large amounts of information and complicated processes that are not grounded in conceptual understanding. Teachers who build their teaching on concepts, regardless of the subject area, can find tasks, questions, and projects for students at many different levels of competence. If, for example, all students in a class understand that stories are built around problems, and if they have examined the ways in which problems are solved in many different stories, they will be able to write structured stories, even though those stories differ greatly in length, technical correctness, and sophistication.

Community in the Classroom

In focusing on academic issues, I have not spoken directly about the social side of school. Yet I have described various situations where disabled students can work with their classmates. Getting any class to the point where exceptional children are accepted as equals by their peers is part of what teachers do as they build a sense of community in their classrooms. This community feeling is reinforced when specialists work in the classroom and aides belong to the classroom, too. *Community* is not a buzzword, but a powerful concept that draws students and adults together in a commitment to their mutual learning, health, and happiness.

Sometimes, community works in unexpected ways. One teacher I observed, who was forming project work groups, spoke openly about the needs of certain students for help or modeling. At first I cringed at this public identification of needy students, but when I saw the groups at work, I realized that class members were responding positively to the teacher's comments. The identified students were being included and helped in the ways the teacher had suggested, without any hostility or put-downs. Children in that class saw themselves as members of the same community and believed that it was the job of community members to help one another.

Preparing for Gifted Students

Much of what I have said about teaching disabled students in regular classrooms applies to gifted students, too. Under the same basic principles, they need to fit in socially and academically, enjoying opportunities to participate, collaborate, work on their own projects, and find their own levels of comfort and challenge. Sometimes, gifted students need help in doing things they are not good at. More often, they can give help to others. You should research the backgrounds of gifted students, just as you do for disabled students, and then prepare their profiles. However, the things to look for in those profiles will be somewhat different. You should be searching for ways to give students more independence rather than more help. These are some questions related to the characteristics of gifted students that you should try to answer:

1. Given that most gifted students have a range of interests, which interests has the student pursued on his own by reading, joining a group, or starting a hobby or a business?

2. What does he do when he finishes class work ahead of the others?

3. Does she often do class work and homework superficially and carelessly as if she doesn't care about what she produces?

4. Does he pursue new interests with speed and enthusiasm, only to abandon them without accomplishing much?

5. Are her friends other gifted children or a mixture of gifted and ordinary children?

6. What social or physical activities, books, movies, television shows, etc. does he enjoy?

All students, but especially gifted ones, ought to have a curriculum that provides a solid foundation and good tools, and then allows them to build their own houses. That is the position on differentiation I have taken throughout this book. And in each chapter I have described structures, strategies, and activities that guide and support students when they are ready to build. Many of the activities suggested are "stretchable" in both directions. With only minor changes, gifted students can use them to express their own interests, greater knowledge, and advanced skills. Yet readers who are familiar with the imagination, independence, and quirkiness of gifted students may wonder if there is anything more or different that teachers can do for those who want to move beyond the curriculum.

Moving Beyond the Curriculum

The answer is, "Yes, get out of their way." The class curriculum, no matter how engaging and challenging, cannot always satisfy the minds and hearts of children who constantly see new doors to open and new paths to travel. My work with children over many years has convinced me that Einstein was right: The signature characteristic of giftedness is curiosity. And curiosity leaps joyously over curricular boundaries without looking back. What I have not yet discussed in this book are the possibilities for differentiated learning outside the curriculum, through leadership, entrepreneurship, and invention.

For students to assume any of these roles in the true sense, the teacher must relinquish some control. Although you cannot allow students to work on special projects unsupervised in the school building, on school time, you can step back and become an advisor, provider, and facilitator while students forge ahead into uncharted territory. In order to better understand how gifted students can become leaders, entrepreneurs, and inventors, let's look at descriptions of some projects that gifted students might choose to undertake.

Leadership, Entrepreneurship, and Invention

One project that seems to fascinate gifted students of any age is starting a newspaper. Since this is not a whole-class project, you should not take class time to teach students how to produce a newspaper, but you should provide the would-be journalists with start-up supplies, allow them to use *journalists*

the class computers and printer, and give them the option of using class silent reading or homework time to get started. You can also let the journalists work in the classroom during recesses or after school. While the newspaper is being created, you are the staff's editorial board. They need to meet with you regularly about the stories they are planning and the editorial positions they are taking. At times, you may have to call their work to a halt if it is heading out of the bounds of legality or propriety. If students have no previous experience with production, you may also have to be their source of technical know-how.

In addition to leadership, a successful newspaper takes creative ideas and entrepreneurship. Someone has to think up new features that will keep readers coming back; someone has to promote the paper so that readers will buy it. But a newspaper also needs reliable and cooperative workers, so the leaders and entrepreneurs will have to recruit, train, monitor, and sustain other students for those jobs. Most student newspapers die out after an issue or two because the leaders lose interest and the work is harder and more routine than they thought. But while the paper lasts, the students involved learn a lot about a complex real-world system and the skills it takes to keep it running. The most important learning for gifted students is that good ideas have to be supported by hard work and attention to details.

②
play

Another appealing project is producing a play. Fairly often, a gifted student will write a play script and want a chance to present it to an audience. You can help by finding a suitable place for practice and presentation, and acting as a chaperone for students working in unsupervised school areas. You can show the playwright/producer how to fill out the school's required paperwork and help him or her figure out costs. You can allow scripts to be typed up and printed in the classroom and some initial readings to go on there. You may also allow some class time to be used for recruiting other students to be part of the project. There are other creative and leadership roles to be filled, and an entrepreneur is also needed to direct the advertising and ticket sales. In addition, plays need behind-the-scenes workers.

As with the newspaper, the teacher needs to hold regular meetings with the project leaders to discuss progress and problems. You may also have to help them get some technical help for lighting and sound. But again, this project belongs to the students who originated it, not the class. Most of the rehearsing, preparing scenery, and making costumes has to be done on the students' own time.

Play production either never gets off the ground—because the playwright can't get enough others to commit to the project—or it proceeds to presentation. Through presentation of their work, the students involved learn about the intricacies of dramatic production: how many people, different skills, costumes, scenery, and props are needed to produce even a simple two-character play. In displaying their special gifts before an audience they also begin to be self-critical, recognizing where they need to improve and learn new skills. If they have a large auditorium to fill or put on more than one performance, they also learn that popular culture sells better than art, and that music and comedy are more attractive to paying customers than serious drama.

Students of all ages often want to get involved in a cause they believe in. Politics, environmental issues, and helping the less fortunate are popular causes that invite gifted students to start projects. The purpose of a project may be to raise awareness, collect money, or to enlist others in service of the cause. Teachers have to be wary of politics; they can't support students in a political cause on school time or with school resources. However, when the cause is charitable, for the benefit of the school, or in the interest of society in general, school time and school supplies can be used. Although initiated by individual students, these projects become whole-class or whole-school projects, involving several leaders and large numbers of workers. In fact, they become an ad-hoc part of the class curriculum.

Projects of this type offer great opportunities for students to lead and create. Some students will want to design posters, buttons, and banners: others will be more interested in thinking up slogans, planning advertisements, and giving speeches. On the other hand, there is also a lot of planning, organizing, and attending to details that elementary and middle school students, no matter how gifted, will need adult help with. For this reason you would be wise to enlist a couple of parents to supervise those parts of the project.

Invention in school is usually a matter of seeing a need or purpose no else sees and inventing a project to serve it. This is another area where gifted students excel. An inventive project might be organizing a crew of older students to teach group games to younger ones on the playground, forming a hobby club to meet during the noon hour, writing a school song or a school cheer, putting together a class yearbook, making a set of math manipulatives out of wood scraps, starting a dancing class after school, or adopting a road near the school to clean up periodically. Since this last project is carried out outside the school and the school day, the teacher again plays an advisory role.

Sometimes gifted students invent objects, too, but those are rarely new creations. More often they are cheaper or more available versions of existing commercial products. I have seen sponges fastened together on a yardstick to clean cafeteria tables, classroom storage cabinets made of plastic bins and mounted on wheels, a kindergarten pocket chart made out of clothing patch pockets sewn onto a quilt, and electric board games. Although inventing objects is not easy, it has the special allure of being a one- or two-person job. Student inventors often like to work alone, but then, like most of us, they want public recognition. When they come up with an object that is interesting and useful and that can be easily produced, they often become the center of class attention and admiration.

Suggestions for Other Projects

There are countless other individual projects gifted students can and will undertake that don't fit neatly under the three role categories I originally named. To give you an idea of their range and variety I will list several possibilities here. What these projects have in common is that they are appealing to—and within the capabilities of—gifted students in elementary and middle schools and they don't require close teacher monitoring.

Planting a school garden or flower beds

Teaching a craft to other students

Making a pop-up book for young children

Making an animated film

Inventing a board game

Constructing word puzzles

Making holiday decorations

Writing a mystery story

Producing a computer PowerPoint display

Writing poetry

Composing and playing music

Making a "how-to" photo album—suitable for teaching others

Learning to perform magic tricks

Making puppets

Storytelling

I want to close this discussion of special projects for gifted students by suggesting that there is at least one way to bring such projects into the mainstream of school activity and regulate them without taking so much extra teacher time and effort. The following vignette describes a school store that has functioned successfully in an elementary school for more than twenty years by selling mainly student-made products. Although the store's entrepreneurs are not all gifted students, the cleverness and quality of most of the products they make exemplify the true essence of giftedness.

The School Store

It's only 11:40 A.M., but already children are trickling out of the lunchroom and lining up outside the room that holds the school store. In ten minutes, grades four/five teacher Nan Youngerman will open the door and let the shoppers in. Inside, several children of all ages are setting up their displays with help from Ms. Youngerman and a couple of her students. Their wares are mostly homemade. Commercial goods—except for things like pencils and erasers—do not sell well here, and Ms. Youngerman encourages children to invent and construct original products.

Behind one display table stands first grader Amy, whose "Fuzzy Worms," cut out of pile fabric with felt eyes and a tongue glued on, have been a top seller for several months. She charges 15 cents apiece for them, with 3 cents (20 percent) going to the store and the rest to her. At another table are Todd and Sam, second graders, who make and sell hand-drawn mazes for 5 cents each. Since they have no material costs, the 4 cents they earn on each maze is all profit. At other tables creator/sellers arrange their goods carefully and put up small price signs. There are various kinds of jewelry: earrings, pins, barrettes, and friendship bracelets; decorated magnets; yarn dolls; pom-poms; and greeting cards. Prices range from 5 cents to 25 cents, although there are a few more elaborate items costing 50 cents to a dollar because they require more work. These expensive things do not sell fast, but they are often chosen when a child is looking for a gift for a friend or relative.

A few of the items for sale are class projects, such as the pancake recipe book written by a second-grade class after reading a book about pancakes for breakfast. In the past other classes have made other kinds of books, decorated stationery, painted paperweights, cookies, and valentine-making kits.

Right now there are no big holidays coming up, but in the various holiday seasons, the school store does great business. Christmas brings a demand for greeting cards, window decorations, and tree ornaments. Valentine's Day encourages candy makers, poets and artists to create lots of salable goods. Halloween masks and small, decorated pumpkins always sell well in October.

At 11:50 Ms. Youngerman opens the store door for a half hour of brisk business. The shoppers rush in to see if there is anything new for sale or if the old favorites are still available. Even a couple of teachers wander in. They may be looking for hand-decorated thank-you notes, a gift for a child, or a pencil with the school name on it. Other times they come into the store just to buy some gift certificates to give to students who have earned a reward for their work or behavior.

By the door sit two fifth graders. One is a cashier, the other records sales so that the sellers can be paid. The coins in the till mount up quickly. No records are kept of individual student profits, but already this year—January—the store has earned about $70, which means that the total sales were close to $350. The real profit, however, is what all the children involved have learned about responsibility, craftsmanship, and the realities of capitalism.

References

BULY, M. R., AND S. VALENCIA. 2003. "Meeting the Needs of Failing Readers: Cautions and Considerations for State Policy." An occasional paper for the University of Washington Center for the Study of Teaching and Policy (April).

CLARK, C., AND R. CALLOW. 2002. *Educating the Gifted and Talented: Resource Issues and Processes for Teachers.* London: David Fulton.

COUGHLIN, D. 2000. *The Mainstreaming Handbook.* Portsmouth, NH: Heinemann.

HEINICH, R. 1979. *Educating All Handicapped Children.* Englewood Cliffs, NJ: Educational Technology Publications.

HYMER, B., AND D. MICHEL. 2002. *Gifted and Talented Learners: Creating a Policy for Inclusion.* London: David Fulton.

STERNBERG, L., R. TAYLOR, AND J. SCHILIT. 1986. *So You're Not a Special Educator: A General Handbook for Educating Handicapped Children.* Springfield, IL: Charles C. Thomas.

STOPPER, M., ED. 2000. *Meeting the Social and Emotional Needs of Gifted and Talented Children.* London: David Fulton.

YATVIN, J. 1982. "Sorting out Gifted Children from Bright Ones." *New York Times.* 14 November.

———. 1992. "Learning to Swim in the Mainstream: Educating Handicapped Children in Regular Classrooms." *Reading in Virginia* (October).

———. 1992. Navigating the Mainstream. *Educational Leadership* (March).

———. 1995. "Flawed Assumptions." *Phi Delta Kappan* 76: 6 (February): 482–84.

10

Finding Support for Yourself as a Differentiating Teacher

As you were reading suggestions for activities, units, grouping, and teaching strategies throughout this book, you probably said to yourself many times, "I already do that." Of course you do. Teachers who believe in differentiating instruction were trying out their own ideas and weaving them into their everyday practice long before this book was conceived. Wherever you are now on the continuum of differentiation, the important thing is to keep adding, modifying, and integrating rich and flexible plans into your literacy program, while deemphasizing, redesigning, and discarding plans that require everyone to do the same thing in the same way in the same length of time. Don't be discouraged by the fact that the differentiation journey is slow and never-ending. That's the way it was meant to be.

The purpose of this chapter is to help you find companionship and support on that journey. One of the largest impediments to the improvement of teaching has always been the physical and intellectual isolation that traditionally go with a teacher's job. To combat that isolation, teachers need other teachers who are moving in the same direction to stimulate their thinking and share their experiences. They also need a constant inflow of new ideas to try out and new materials to work with. This chapter will discuss both the common and the uncommon sources of support available.

Mental
filter

Developing a Mental Filter

Your most loyal companion will be a mental filter that operates almost auto-matically to help you identify promising ideas you can adopt or adapt for your own classroom. A mental filter is a quick decision maker that lets you know whether or not an educational idea fits with your philosophy and style of teaching. As with any cognitive structure, a mental filter cannot be described in words. But I can list some of the questions your filter should be running through whenever you meet a new idea for differentiating instruc-tion. All the answers will merge into a holistic "yes" or "no" decision about the idea's appropriateness for your students.

For stud 1

Does the idea offer my students

rich content that will capture their interest and expand their horizons?

several different possibilities for levels of performance?

a high degree of independence in choosing and carrying out their work?

structural models to help them stay on track?

reasonable expectations for time, materials, and skills?

checkpoints for decision making, self-regulation, and self-criticism?

For Teacher

Does the idea allow me, as a teacher,

to give explanations and instructions to the whole class?

to work with small groups and individual students that need my help?

to supervise and monitor student work without feeling overwhelmed?

to delegate some responding, suggesting, and editing responsibilities to students or other adults?

In essence, what your mental filter is trying to identify for you are ideas that have learning value, are practical for classrooms, are appealing to your students, and give students a balance between freedom and control.

Working with Colleagues

Once your mental filter is in place, you can begin to sort out ideas from the resources available in your environment. The resource most accessible for most teachers is the fellowship of colleagues in their school. When like-minded teachers think together, they become more creative and resourceful than when they are alone. In many schools teachers working at the same grade level or teaching the same subject have a regular time at school to meet for planning. If the group meets once a week, they can set aside one meeting a month specifically to share ideas for differentiating instruction, although they shouldn't push any ideas aside if they pop up at other times. The purpose of designating a time for talking about differentiation is to make sure that it doesn't get overlooked.

When a new idea for differentiating is brought up, the teachers who like the way it sounds may volunteer to try it out, making whatever changes they feel are necessary. Those with reservations may wait and see. At the following month's meeting the experimenters can report on their results, and everyone can discuss the pros, cons, and possible modifications. Ideas that have worked for at least one teacher should be recorded in a notebook, along with space for comments from future experimenters. Such a notebook will be a good resource for new teachers and continuing teachers when they feel they are running dry.

Better than hearing or reading about a new idea, however, is seeing it played out in a classroom with real students. If teachers are willing to give up a planning period once in a while, taking the opportunity to observe a colleague is tremendously rewarding. In my own career, I have learned more from watching teachers teach than from any other source. There has always been something I could use or adapt—or decide I would never do again. In schools where teachers are physically and intellectually isolated, however, it may be difficult to find people willing to be observed. Isolated teachers sometimes grow distrustful of one another. Under such circumstances, you may have to go elsewhere. If your school district provides "professional days" for its teachers, or your principal is willing to release you for a day, you can visit another school where you have friends or where you've heard that teachers are doing exciting things and welcoming visitors.

Teachers in schools where teachers do not plan together and have few opportunities to talk informally with one another about their practice may have to seek collegiality at other times and in other places. Often, there are informal study groups of teachers that meet after school or in the evening to read and discuss the same professional books. These groups could also devote some time to sharing ideas and experiences in differentiation. In addition, there are probably university courses offered nearby, organized as seminars, that operate through discussion. To choose the right course for you, look in university catalogues for titles and descriptions that promise discussion of school renewal and change. Also examine the course syllabi and reading lists. Look for discussion topics that are interesting and reading lists with book titles that are new and provocative. If possible, get a friend to take the course with you so you can talk about it going to and from class.

Wider Collegiality

Collegiality on a wider geographical basis can be found through school district inservice sessions, professional organizations, and the Internet. Most school districts hold inservice training days during the school year, and the more affluent ones offer voluntary workshops over the summer. Whatever the topics of these inservice sessions, there are almost always a couple of ideas for differentiation included. But even if you don't come away with ideas you can use, you are likely to meet teachers from other schools who are also seeking to further differentiate their practice. Don't let them get away without making plans to get together and talk about your mutual interests.

National and state organizations customarily hold annual conferences you can attend and have committees you can join. The larger organizations may also convene special-interest groups where people who feel strongly about a particular aspect of their profession can get together and form collegial attachments that can be sustained through email. In addition, several well-known authors and researchers have established their own websites or listservs to share their work and opinions with interested educators. They are happy to have you sign on. You can read their messages, go to the references they cite, and communicate with them directly. A short list of organization websites is provided in the references at the end of this chapter. For author websites, go to Google.com and type in an author's name.

Professional Materials

Because we can never tell where teaching ideas may be lying in wait for us, we need to be open to all kinds of print, visual displays, and electronic media—with our mental filters turned on. Professional organizations publish books, newsletters, journals, and videos directed toward specific areas of interest and, often, particular philosophies of education. Some organizations also sell audio tapes of outstanding presentations at their conferences. Good ideas show up regularly in teachers' magazines and books on teaching that are not connected with any organization. Never pass by a book or an article that addresses the teaching of literacy in general or differentiated instruction in particular without looking at its introduction and thumbing through its pages. At least pause when you run across materials on "learning styles," "multiple intelligences," "closing the learning gap," "higher-order thinking skills," or something similar. There is a good possibility that descriptions of differentiated activities will be included.

At the same time, don't ignore ordinary newspapers, magazines, and other non-professional sources. We all know that *National Geographic* is a great reference source for scientific and geographical information that students can use, but we may forget to look through *Scientific American, Time, Newsweek,* and the science and travel sections of our local newspapers. Even all those advertisements that we skip over without reading may be valuable as models for school writing. Students can design their own products and present them in formats and language taken from the newspaper ads. By the same token, television commercials can serve as models for student-made commercials.

As a faithful reader of the newspaper comics pages, I have also found material for differentiated activities in puzzles and comics. In "The Family Circus," for example, the child characters often mis-define adult words they've heard. I think that real children in school would have fun deliberately doing the same with multisyllabic words taken from the dictionary. Awhile ago, the comic "Luann" devoted several strips to the process of two students working together to write a play for their English class. Those strips could be used as an introduction to collaborative play writing in a middle school classroom. Classroom sequences from "Peanuts" remind me what children sometimes think of school and how oblivious teachers can be to children's feelings. However, I think the best use of comics for differentiation is to have children write their own dialogue and paste it over the original words in the balloons. They can tell the same story as the comic in their own way or change it outrageously by putting very different words into the characters' mouths.

In fairness to textbooks and their teachers' guides, I must add them to my list of sources. Although these commercial items are almost always written on the premise that "one size fits all," they sometimes include suggestions for differentiated activities or describe activities that you can differentiate with only small changes.

Getting Ideas from Students

One source of ideas that teachers may overlook is their own students. Children can tell you a lot about topics they want to study and how to differentiate them, and they will understand if their teacher has to make minor changes to render activities suitable for classrooms use. Choosing a lull between units, prime the pump for discussion by asking students about activities and projects they have already done that would be fun to do again with different content. Or ask students to brainstorm new activities they'd like to try. To help things along, you can suggest categories such as persuasive writing, research, or poetry and have students supply the specifics. As the class winnows its lists down to their favorite ideas, remind them that they want activities that will allow lots of choices yet have enough controls built in to give them the support they need.

Student feedback after an activity or unit is also valuable. Ask specific questions, such as:

How could this activity have been changed to give you more freedom and/or more guidance?

Can you think of topics to read or write about that you would have found more interesting?

Could we have organized groups differently for more effective collaboration?

Promise to listen and consider suggestions, but explain that you won't be able to do everything that everyone wants. Sandwiched in between the gripes and the wild ideas there will always be gems that may make learning easier and more lasting for your students.

Using Your Inner Resources

Finally, teachers need to look for ideas within themselves. Although action research has become a cliche in our profession, that fact doesn't diminish its value as a source for improving teacher practice. Action research is really only the formalization of what creative teachers have always done: trying out new things and evaluating the results. If you need numbers to prove to yourself and others that a new idea works, formalize your plan with a pretest, posttest, time frame, and treatment fidelity. You may be able to persuade another teacher to let you use his class as your control group. But if you believe that good teachers know success when they see it, be informal in your approach. It would be helpful, however, to have a colleague observe your teaching and discuss what they saw with you. Even the best teachers are not aware of everything that happens in their classrooms.

Reflection is another way of looking inside yourself. Good teachers think about their teaching afterward as well as planning for it beforehand. That's why they rarely teach a unit or activity exactly the way they did the first time. Although, as I said above, teachers do not see everything while they are teaching, they do notice widespread boredom, confusion, or resentment among their students. And teachers can see when the quality of the work students produce is far below what they had hoped for. Reflection helps teachers to figure out what went wrong and fix it. It enables them to reteach, to give extra help to those who need it, to adjust the pace of their teaching, to bring in more models, to expand guided practice, and, sometimes, to start over. For teachers who are trying to fit instruction to students, reflection is a powerful resource.

Nevertheless, there is a danger in reflection that makes it unwise for teachers to rely on it solely. In working with early career teachers, I observe them teaching a class and write up my reactions to what I see. At the same time, I ask the teachers to write their own reactions to the lesson I observed and send it to me before they receive mine. Almost always there are discrepancies between the two reflections, with me seeing much more that needs to be fixed than the teachers do. These discrepancies may be a side effect of my natural grumpiness. They may be the result of differences in philosophy—with me being far behind the times. Or they may just represent the difference between the roles of evaluator and the one being evaluated, with teachers afraid to reveal weaknesses that perhaps I didn't notice. Maybe all of these explanations are valid, but I think something else is happening too: denial. Psychologically, when we choose something and make it ours—in this case, a teaching method, a style, a lesson—it is very hard to disown it and, in so doing, diminish our view of ourselves. If, indeed, this psychological phenomenon is operating whenever teachers reflect on their practice, they need to balance reflection with another perspective. One way to get that perspective is to open their classrooms to colleagues and to take seriously the critical comments of principals and other outside evaluators. Although outsiders cannot learn much about you, your class, or what has come before from only one short visit, they see what they see. If you have doubts about their perceptions, you can follow up by videotaping yourself doing a similar lesson and then trying to view it through the eyes of an outsider.

Pacing Change

In using any of these resources to improve your ability to differentiate, you should follow the oft-given advice—move slowly. Today, more than ever, teachers have so many responsibilities and so many masters to answer to that going full bore into big changes in practice foreshadows failure. Wisdom dictates that teachers try one type of differentiation at a time, and then in a small way. For instance, a teacher who has been using one novel with the whole class should go to two novels and two groups before creating five groups and assigning five different books. As another example, a teacher should start cooperative learning—even if students have used it in previous classes—with well-defined group roles; short, specific tasks; and lots of group reflection on them before allowing students to embark on extended projects. Another reason not to do too much at once or to go too deeply into a type of activity or unit right away is that it is harder to make adjustments in big things than in small ones. One constant we can count on in teaching is that adjustments always have to be made.

Sustaining Differentiated Instruction

As I indicated at the beginning of this chapter, the process of becoming a differentiating teacher is recursive—a never-ending journey. Any and all of the sources described above will help to keep you going and growing throughout your career. It would be wonderful if all teachers could teach in schools where differentiation was the mode, where everyone—and that includes the principal—was continually working to make a better fit between each child and his learning. But even though it is harder for a teacher working alone to find the stimulation and support she needs, a network of collegial relationships and the strength of self-knowledge will sustain her. The term "differentiated instruction" may be just a brief fad in the history of education, but the principle behind it is eternal. What educators—whether teachers in schools or parents in homes—have always known is that the mysterious process we call learning is different for every child.

References

DUDLEY-MARLING, C. 1997. *Living with Uncertainty: The Messy Reality of Classroom Practice.* Portsmouth, NH: Heinemann.

LIEBERMAN, A., AND L. MILLER. 1984. *Teachers, Their World and Their Work: Implications for School Improvement.* Alexandria, VA: Association for Supervision and Curriculum Development.

MYERS, M. 1985. *The Teacher Researcher: How to Study Writing in the Classroom.* Urbana, IL: The National Council of Teachers of English.

Organization Websites

International Reading Association—www.ira.org

National Reading Conference—www.nrconline.org

National Council of Teachers of English—www.ncte.org

American Library Association—www.ala.org

American Educational Research Association—www.aera.net

Special Education and Gifted Student References

CLARK, C., R. CALLOW. 2002. *Educating the Gifted and Talented: Resource Issues and Processes for Teachers.* London: David Fulton Publishers.

COUGHLIN, D. 2000. *The Mainstreaming Handbook.* Portsmouth, NH: Heinemann.

HEINICH, R. 1979. *Educating All Handicapped Children.* Educational Technology Publications: Englewood Cliffs, NJ.

HYMER, B., D. MICHEL. 2002. *Gifted and Talented Learners: Creating a Policy for Inclusion.* London: David Fulton Publishers.

STERNBERG, L., R. TAYLOR, AND J. SCHILIT. 1986. *So You're Not a Special Educator: A General Handbook for Educating Handicapped Children.* Springfield, IL: Charles C. Thomas.

STOPPER, M., ED. 2000. *Meeting the Social and Emotional Needs of Gifted and Talented Children.* London: David Fulton Publishers.

YATVIN, J. 1982. "Sorting out Gifted Children from Bright Ones." *New York Times.* 14 November.

———. 1992. "Navigating the Mainstream." *Educational Leadership* (March).

———. 1992. *Learning to Swim in the Mainstream: Educating Handicapped Children in Regular Classrooms.* Reading in Virginia (October).

———. 1995. "Flawed Assumptions." *Phi Delta Kappan* 76, no. 6 (February): 482–84.

List of Poetry Books

ADOFF, A., illus. E. A. McCully. 2002. *Black Is Brown Is Tan.* New York: HarperCollins.

ADOFF, A. 1979. *Eats.* New York: Lothrop, Lee & Shepard.

ATTENBOROUGH, L., ed. 2001. *Poetry by Heart—A Child's Book of Poems to Remember.* New York: Scholastic.

CARLE, E., illus., and L. Whipple, comp. 1999. *Eric Carle's Animals, Animals.* New York: Puffin.

DEREGNIERS, B., ed., various Caldecott illus. 1988. *Sing a Song of Popcorn: Every Child's Book of Poems.* Reprinted. New York: Scholastic.

DE LA MARE, W. 2003. *Rhymes and Verses: Collected Poems for Young People.* New York: Holt.

DUNNING, S., E. LUEDERS, AND H. SMITH. 1967. *Reflections on a Gift of Watermelon Pickle and Other Modern Verse.* New York: Lothrop, Lee & Shepard.

FLORIAN, D. 2002. *Summersaults.* New York: Greenwillow.

____. 2003. *Bow Wow Meow Meow: It's Rhyming Cats and Dogs.* New York: Harcourt.

GREENBERG, J. 2001. *Heart to Heart: New Poems Inspired by Twentieth-Century American Art.* New York: Abrams.

HALL, D. 2001. *The Oxford Illustrated Book of American Children's Poems.* Oxford, United Kingdom: Oxford University Press.

HUGHES, L., AND L. B. 1969. *Don't You Turn Back.* New York: Knopf.

____. 2001. *A Poke in the I: A Collection of Concrete Poems.* Cambridge, MA: Candlewick.

JANECZKO, P. B., illus. C. Raschka. 1981. *Don't Forget to Fly: A Cycle of Modern Poetry.* New York: Atheneum.

_____. 2002. *Seeing the Blue Between–Advice and Inspiration for Young Poets.* Cambridge, MA: Candlewick Press.

KENNEDY, X. J., AND D. M. KENNEDY, illus. J. Dyer. 1992. *Talking Like the Rain–A Read-to-Me Book of Poems.* Boston, MA: Little, Brown.

KENNEDY, X. J., AND D. M. illus. K. L. Baker. 1999. *Knock at a Star–A Child's Introduction to Poetry.* Reprint ed. Boston, MA: Little, Brown.

KOCH, K., AND K. FARRELL. 1981. *Sleeping on the Wing: An Anthology of Modern Poetry with Essays on Reading and Writing.* New York: Random House.

KUSKIN, K., illus. S. Ruzzier. 2003. *Moon, Have You Met My Mother?: The Collected Poems of Karla Kuskin.* New York: HarperCollins.

LARRICK, N. 1977. *Crazy to be Alive in Such a Strange World: Poems About People.* New York: M. Evans & Co.

LIVINGSTON, M. C. 1979. *O Sliver of Liver, and Other Poems.* New York: Atheneum.

LYNE, S., ed., illus. J. Monks. 2004. *Soft Hay Will Catch You–Poems by Young People.* New York: Simon & Schuster.

MERRIAM, E. 1964. *It Doesn't Always Have to Rhyme.* New York: Atheneum.

PRELUTSKY, J., ed., illus. Arnold Lobel. 2000. *The Random House Book of Poetry for Children.* Reprint ed. New York: Random House.

PRELUTSKY, J., ed., illus. M. So. 1999. *The 20th Century Children's Poetry Treasury.* New York: Knopf.

ROGASKY, B., ed., illus. T. S. Hyman. 1999. *Winter Poems.* Reprint ed. New York: Scholastic.

ROSEN, M., ed., illus. B. Graham. 1993. *Poems for the Very Young.* New York: Kingfisher.

ROSEN, M., ed., illus. P. Howard. 1998. *Classic Poetry–An Illustrated Collection.* Cambridge, MA: Candlewick.

SILVERSTEIN, S. 2004. 30th anniversary special ed. *Where the Sidewalk Ends: Poems and Drawings.* New York: HarperCollins.

STEPTOE, J. 2001. *In Daddy's Arms I Am Tall: African Americans Celebrating Fathers.* New York: Lee & Low.

UNTERMEYER, L., ed., illus. by J. W. Anglund. 1998. *The Golden Books Family Treasury of Poetry.* New York: Golden Books.

UPDIKE, J., illus. T. S. Hyman. 1999. *A Child's Calendar.* New York: Holiday House.

VECCHIONE, P., ed. 2002. *Whisper and Shout–Poems to Memorize.* Chicago: Cricket Books.

VIORST, J. 1981. *If I Were in Charge of the World and Other Worries: Poems for Children and Their Parents.* New York: Atheneum.

_____. 1995. *Sad Underwear and Other Complications.* New York: Aladdin.

WILLIAMS, V. B. 2001. *Amber Was Brave, Essie Was Smart: The Story of Amber and Essie Told Here in Poems and Pictures.* New York: Greenwillow.

ZEMACH, M. 2001. *Some from the Moon, Some from the Sun: Poems and Songs for Everyone.* New York: Farrar, Straus & Giroux.

Index